THE UNGODLY: My Experience with the Devil

A very true story

Copyright © 2017

All rights reserved by copyright owner.

This work may be freely distributed.

First Edition: May 2017

Printed in the United States of America

ISBN: 978-0-9978473-2-1

Library of Congress Control #2017905572

Deuteronomy 11:18-19

"Therefore shall ye lay up these My words in your heart and in your soul and bind them for a sign upon your hand that they may be as frontlets between your eyes.

And **ye shall teach them your children,** speaking of them when thou sittest in thine house, and when thou walkest by the way, when thou liest down, and when thou risest up."

Note: Usually, when I say "Lord", it's interchangeable and THEY know who I'm addressing when I'm speaking to them, but for readers' sake, in this book when I say "Lord", I mean Jesus. When I say "God" I mean the one God.

I get the feeling later in this memoir, HE will be Father because HE keeps reiterating that to me. HE told me we're HIS babies. There are God-fearing people who are sensitive about the "Father" thing because HE's GOD, though I know folks of other Abrahamic religions have heard HIM say it to them even if it's not okay in their circles to admit it.

Isa – Jesus in Islam

He – Jesus

HE, HIM – God

- *God is just always right behind me because this sucka is always on my heels. A dream. That's how it started. Well, almost.*

9 Years ago

He snatched the gas nozzle from my hand because I didn't want his help. It was a cold afternoon. I had just left work and I was tired.

We stared at one another – me insecure and wanting him to go away, and him heavy-handed and insistent with a bulbous head and one milky, blind eye. I allowed him to pump my gas, avoided his play for conversation and then drove myself home – forgetting him the moment I turned onto the highway.

Then I was dozing on the couch after

work. The house was cold, so I had laid down still wearing my coat. I awoke with a jolt when I saw that white, milky eye behind my eyelids, and the Lord's voice was loud. He said, "Every time I awake, Satan is in your backyard. He had better leave you alone or I'm gonna beat his MOTHERFUCKING ASS!"

I know what you're thinking. God doesn't speak those terrible words. That's what I would've said too.

He also said…louder and angrier. "And tell him I said that if he keeps trying to raise the dead I'm going to break his…"

Right. So…

This is my life.

I wasn't always wonderful (heh). I didn't always know God. But even when I was a bad girl, Satan would call me a "bitch". Bitch, bitch, bitch. I would hiss. Fight. Scream.

I knew Jesus first. He would stop in periodically to see if I was ready for repentance. When I was, He worked with me. The voices started about four years ago and grew more noticeable after trauma.

Because I pray all day, from morning to night, I figured it was God talking to me. When the voices brought words that made me feel insecure, I thought it was chastening - that I was doing something wrong. I was an old sinner which sometimes equaled to me "no salvation"; that God wouldn't forgive me for certain things. Every bad thing I did equaled no salvation - to me. I knew what repentance was, but somehow felt that it wasn't really *for me*. I forgot that God is LOVE. Why would my God build me up only to tear me down?

That's when I started to wonder - asked God - what is that voice with the quick insults? The condemning and put downs?

When Jesus came to help me repair, I felt weighed down by guilt. God came to get to know me and I fell in love with HIM, and of course eventually, I had to deal with grief.

It seemed that trauma after trauma came - a broken heart, attack from co-workers, a sexually assaulted friend, and on and on. Things that bothered me that were once "out of sight, out of mind" weighed on my brain - child molesters which I detest, a video of a young girl's rape by a police officer remaining online even until this day, a photo of a child's face while being molested, stumbling across a video on Facebook of a little girl being groomed by her mother to have sex with a grown man, a toddler masturbating…

When I asked God why people hurt children – hurt other people – HE told me plainly that they were demons. Rapists are demons. Murderer – demon. Child molester – demon.

I had a friend once who told me that a demon was in her brother. I nodded and told her to pray. In my mind, demons were the little girls in movies possessed by evil spirits – ugly, smelly, contorting parasites that could only be vanquished with the help of a good priest because their mothers had no belief in the Almighty God. Demons smile, play games, tell you kind words, and try to trick you but they're dumb. That was me.

But no. Demons walk side by side with us every day – sometimes arm in arm.

Anything that bothered me popped up. I felt as if I were being attacked. I retreated to gain my bearings, but still I had no idea what was wrong. When I heard stories of people who had fought with the devil, I nodded and shook my head.

Satan coming in dreams and fighting or coercing women into sex – I would shake my head. That could never happen to me. Never. Not that he had never accosted me in a dream. Quite the opposite, in fact. But if I called Jesus, He was always there and the problem would disappear.

Jesus. Anyone who knows me knows that I love Jesus. Jesus this and Jesus that. I can't see Him but I know He's around. Unlike God who is a provider and excellent for comfort, Jesus is more like a friend.

GOD CALLED ME

I was busy making arrangements - arrangements that I didn't want my mother to worry about. I was afraid of the afterlife though I had been assured that I would be okay.

This new presence - the sexual stuff - started in the bathroom while I showered. Me being me, I figured it was Jesus since I talk to Him all the time. So me, "Jesus this and Lord that".

He said something that made me upset. After I got into bed is when the voice started. I had a vision of the Lord beating me. When I say a vision, I mean there was no physical contact but there was definitely spiritual contact. Satan beat the hell out of me and I thought it was the Lord so my customary fighting, cursing and thrashing was non-existent. I would not raise a hand to the Lord or curse Him, so I got my head "crashed in" that's how I saw it.

This event was so traumatic to me that I tried to block God and the Lord's voice, and so much so that I planned to go to a Buddhist Temple to block this "voice". I did not want to hear. I was afraid. I thought THEY were trying to kill me.

Never before had I experienced this. Why would I think it was the devil when he had barely been allowed to speak to me before without divine intervention? In my mind, Christ was spitting hateful words and He had hit me so hard that I would've sworn that He held a sledgehammer. I was sick to my soul. I did not call for God. In my mind, I had done something so foul – so disrespectful in back talking God that

Christ's excuse was to blot my name from the Book (which He did in my sight).

Now while I lay getting the hell beat out of me, God came and gathered me up, made me safe, and gave me the Prayer of Manasseh. By this time, I wouldn't talk to Christ because I refused to let the devil trick me again. Hell lasted for two weeks while God helped me to differentiate between the voices. The spitting, hateful, malicious voice was none other than that rotten dog.

Then I understood - kinda. Weeks before God had told me that something wanted to rape me, but didn't want me to see it. I thought it was a man.

That was how he tried to worm his way into my life by using something I fear against me > Christ trying to have sex with me; Christ calling me a nappy headed nigra; Christ calling me a whore.

Jesus said to me,

"How did you believe that was me? Why would I waste my time working with you? Why would I hurt something that loves God?"

Guilt.

But all I could say is, "Lord, to cover up that he couldn't act totally like you, he beat my ass and played on my emotions. If it makes you feel any better, he had some jacked up hair."

Now God is always sweet to me. HE makes sure I have money to buy dresses, that I eat, that I have a place to go when I'm extra confused (more than "I need Jesus" confused), and HE tells me which way to go. But HE doesn't seem to sit in one place for very long. All HE says is, "I'm right here."

HE doesn't understand the heart attack either, and I'm more of a dramatic person. "Heart attack" meaning, when danger is near don't call God first, pull out the pistol.

So Jesus is gone and I have God and that's fine. I'm embarrassed to know that the devil has been in my shower - has made sexual advances toward me. I know a woman who had sex with him willingly a few times and all I can wonder is how and why because he is disgusting, but I guess if he plays like he's someone you love… I don't know.

HE said, "Why didn't you call me?"

Guilt.

So even today while I'm writing this, the bastard is walking around spitting obscenities. It's funny the things that you don't think about - the mayhem he provokes makes you think that he's simply evil, we shrug our shoulders at his reputation and move on. But when I'm sitting in my chair and God is talking to me and Satan is being vile to HIM and I'm shocked because the realization finally hits me that he hates the Father God…

Is very disrespectful to HIM to the point that I'm ashamed though the words didn't even come from my mouth. This goes beyond an "Angel Berry tantrum".

It's vile name calling, sexual molestation of Jesus with his clothes split and bleeding up the back, sliding toward the throne hog-tied like an animal.

But alas, he is not the bump in the night. No, no. God is.

Because he doesn't want you to know!

Why would God tell us we will be

forgiven if we repent if HE doesn't mean it? HE is glad when we learn from our mistakes and seek repentance with a true heart. But Satan desires to situate himself into our lives - sometimes in the form of something we covet to proceed to tear down first our faith and then our person.

Abusive spouse? Satan. Anyone who loves you would not harm you. Been raped? Satan. Child missing? Demons.

The way I see it from <u>my experience</u> is whatever you do wrong - whatever sins you've committed, he will use the guilt against you to make you think it will stop God from loving you - that is if you feel guilty about it because feeling guilt is a form of repentance. If one didn't care or recognize their sin, who cares what HE says?

It's natural to want a relationship with God, our maker, but he (the devil) wants you to curse God; he is very disrespectful to God; he wants to shame and hurt HIM through you. God told me he (the devil) sits beneath us and watches our lips move.

He is a God imposter. He will tell you good things to fool you. He will try to weigh you down and steer you into doing what he wants you to do because he is not respected like God where he can make a request and it's done. He will work on your insecurities. When you're strong in the spirit of God, he will try to hurt you. Don't say, "This won't happen to me". He will feed you negativity; he breeds ignorance in God through distractions of sex, distractions in the church, money, greed – all to distract you from the Word of God. He will try to exploit your weaknesses.

Say *Hallelujah*.

It only takes two seconds to screw up anything – meaning our life, state of being, the life of someone else.

One split second.

I'm an adulterer, liar, blah. God knows our heart, but he (the devil) wants us to believe that our sins are so bad that God won't forgive us.

Because I have a mouth like a sailor, I love this example:

~Isaiah 6:5
"…woe is me! For I am undone; because I am a man of unclean lips, and I dwell in the midst of a people of unclean lips: for mine eyes have seen the King, the LORD of hosts."

And of course King David whom God loved:

2 Samuel 11:2
"…David arose from off his bed and walked upon the roof of the king's house…he saw a woman washing herself…the woman was very beautiful…"

2 Samuel 11:4
"…and David sent messengers and took her…and he lay with her…"
2 Samuel 11:5
"And the woman conceived…"
2 Samuel 11:15
"Set ye Uriah (Bathsheba's husband) in the forefront of battle…retire ye from him…that he may be smitten and die."
David repented and followed God until he died.

Love God. CALL GOD

I began this memoir over a week after I realized that the devil had attempted to situate himself into my life. That day was March 16th and this memoir was started March 23rd. It also contains accounts of others who have had similar experiences. It will follow a short story called The Humble, which was published in 2016. It was my way of expressing a strange experience that I could not explain by use of a character named Hattie Mae Cline.

THE HUMBLE
`A short tale from the anthology Telling Really Tall Tales`

"Therefore to him that knoweth to do good, and doeth it not, to him it is sin." James 4:17

(Inspired by a true story)

My name is Hattie Mae Cline and I am eighty-three years old. I'se born in the year 1893 on a cotton plantation in Mississippi. My pa was a sharecropper on Mr. Joe Michaels' land. My ma and pa had nine chillun', three girls and six boys. I'se the eldest chile.

Well, my ma was a woman what had religion. She made sho' all us chillun' known 'bout the savior, bless His heart.

I was a chile who was wild, honey. I was young and beautiful, slender and big breasted, the color of warm honey with big, brown eyes and long legs. I like to go out to the juke joints and dance and holla, listen to jazz and drink that moonshine wit' a little reefer. I'd hang 'round wit' a different fella almost every night – white or black -- and they put in my hand whateva I asked for. So that's the way I went on for a while there.

I ain't forget none what my ma had told me. Always

when I laid down at night the Lord would say to me, Hattie, what are you doing? I would always mean to do better but I was having fun, honey, and that likker had me.

Slowly but surely, He wore me down though'. One time I remembers I went and got me some money from a man, right, and I tell you soon as I get home and lay on my bed to rest didn't the spirit jump right on me! I knows what it was cause I got this hard buzzing all through my body. Ain't another feeling like it. Did I do right after that? Nope. So the Lord got more rigorous. *What's your name*, He would say to me at night. *Hattie*, I'd tell'em. Did He forget me? He was forgetting who I was! *I'm Hattie Mae Cline, Lord*! I lay there and fell asleep worried, honey.

Once I was there in the darkest dark I had known and the Lord said, Hattie, do you want to die? I guess, I told Him. Well, I started to fall fast into the abyss – what's the word? Plummet. I began to plummet into the abyss so fast that my heart dropped. No, no, I screamed – and just like that I awoke and, chile, I knew where I had been on my way to. I hear a suffering voice say, Oh, Hattie, I can't take this for eternity. Hattie, I wish you could feel one drop. One drop of damnation! Lord, Lord! And it ain't no God in hell. No more talking to my Jesus? I can't live like that, I say. And so I began to follow the path as it's written here a little, there a little. It whatn't none easy neither. The Lord was mad at me, but he chastened me wit' love though', chile. Now I'm gone leave some stuff out what's only 'tween me and the Lord, but He supported me and helped me put one foot in front of the otha'. And then I had to forgive myself as well. Ain't no excuse for living like a heathen on purpose.

    Well, He lived wit' me after while and He neva left. We goes on like that still, me stumbling and the Lord grabbing me afore I fall. Same been true throughout history. When folks get to pointing they fingers I say, oh no, King David was a righteous man, but he killed a man for his wife and God forgive him; Paul murdered followers of Christ 'til the Good Lord showed him the way, but folks be just a pointin' and got filth in they closets piled up high.

Now let's talk about the flip side. Just like there's God, there's also a devil and he is mean for sin, chile. My ma used to say he eat feces. Lucifer will attack anything God loves just to hurt Him.

I remembers this one time I'se dozing in my bed and a demon jumped on me. This was 'round the time I'se just starting to try and get myself together. I opened my eyes 'cause sumthin' was on me heavy and I was a fightin' and a scratchin'. I throws it off me and I was a hissin' like a she-cat and that thing fled. I surprised myself how I fought.

Another time I dreamt I'se in a room and there that devil was molesting a woman against the wall. Poor thing, I'll neva forget her. I'se scared to death. I looks to my right and I sees one them dolls what look like a raggedy ann – big though', tall as me sitting in a rocking chair. It had big, black buttons for eyes and its mouth was stitched on and it was beckoning to me. My Lord! I hopped on His lap and we rocked there together and He says to me that if I eva' see the devil just look over and He gone be right there. Well, my word! I sho' appreciate it, Lord.

Well, I continued on the path. The Lord would say, Hattie, follow me. I'se obedient to the Lord 'cause He tells you the right way to go and who to deal wit'. It's your own choice if you don't listen. He tell you straight up too. Ain't no pussyfootin' around – ain't His way.

I prayed and prayed and I talked to the Lord all day everyday – when I was going here and going there, and doing this and doing that. I seek his counsel in everything, chile, and I swears He got the best advisin'.

Anyway, I had darn near stop screwin'. Jesus was working his magic and I ain't won't nobody touchin' me. I was still sippin' on that shine though' 'cause I knew soon He was gone chase that off too. Sho' nuff, He says, Hattie, you gone stop that drinking for three months. Three months? Who was gone do that? Humph!

He got them three months out me though' and didn't that devil try and tempt me in the last days and God send a believer to strengthen me? She said, naw, sista, we gone drink apeoplee juice. Thank you, Lord. After them three months I was just fine, honey. But now I got to be rid of my tobacco. Cut me a break, Lord! Can't do nuthin' 'round here, I stumps off. Do that, go here, talk to this person, don't talk to that person – and He ain't gone leave me alone about my tobacco? What's next, I thoughught? Stop gossipin', Hattie, He comes back. My word!

    Well, like always when you loves the Lord here come the devil. So I'se laying on the couch one night. It was cold outside and I'se all wrapped up warm to the neck in a blanket. I'se dozin' and I remembers feeling real cozy. All of a sudden I gets a hard yank on the foot! I hurry up and looks down and I don't see nuthin so I gets comfortable again. Suddenly I feels two strong hands wrap theyselves 'round my ankles and damn near drag me off the couch. I grabs the back of the couch wit' my hands and gets myself into a sittin' position and me and that devil fought like that wit' him trying to drag me down into water. Yes, yes. My feet was in water and he was trying to pull me down in it. I got to 'renched a leg loose and got to kickin' him all in the head hard as I could. I was furious! Then all of a sudden I'm in midair right there in the living room.

The only time I had been threw in the air in my sleep was when the Lord came in my dreams and toss me around sometimes. He would throw me and toss me and I'd just relax 'cause wasn't much I could do about it. He wanted me to trust Him that He wouldn't let my head hit the wall. This thing here wasn't the Lord. This was a huge serpent that was wrapped around my body and he was squeezing me. He was trying to bind me. The rage I felt! I got to kickin' and cussin' and then I heard one word – PRAY. Just that simple. So I started, Our Father, who art in heaven, hallowed be thine name…And that wicked dog dropped me. I got up and dusted myself off and then woke up sitting right there on the couch. My word!

I'll say one thing, I don't know why the Lord called me. I'm stubborn as all hell; will do anything to pick a fight with a bully; I cusses like a sailor; and I only love followers of our Lord. God wants us to spread His word but I agrees wit' Jonah. Humph! If we don't put forth an effort to have a relationship wit' our God, it's not His loss.

Woman gone tell me one time wit' spite that it ain't no

God. See, this was one of them unbelievers that's used to a Christian that wants to convince them about the glory of the Lord. Not me. I told that woman I don't care what you believe. You betta get your wicked ass away from me.

Lord says to turn the otha' cheek cause vengeance belong to Him. I'ma turn my cheek awrite and that whole side of my body wit' it so when I swing that momentum from the turn gives my fist the right amount of power to knock they teeth out.

Many are called but few are chosen and the connection ain't for everybody. That's what I tells the Lord. I tells Him, Lord, folks wanna do what they wanna do and they don't want no holy structure 'cause then they gots to mend they ways. Some folks is wicked to they heart. Lord, concentrate on the ones that love you. That's how I sees it. People ain't been right to Him since the beginning. He don't ask for much. It burns Him up to see folks chasing after otha' gods and it burns me up that He care 'bout'em. Jesus bled his precious blood for us and we still gotta chase them suckas? Pssh. I can't chase somebody what done heard the same stories I have. If you want to deny your Maker, fine wit' me. I ain't no recruiter. To each his own is what I say. I know the Lord don't like that, but I ain't perfect.

DAILY NOTES
March 16th – May 11th, 2017

"God told me it was alright if I wanted to come home – that He loved me. Afterward, the Lord told me to gird up myself…"

March 16th, 2017

I was still making preparations, getting rid of stuff. I was putting a doll on eBay and was thinking - talking to the Lord - and got irritated about something "He" said and didn't want to talk anymore. It seemed to me that His spirit was irritated for no reason.

I was drinking before bed. That's when the obscenities started - I had blasphemed God, I was a slut, tramp, blotted from the book.

I remember a vision of standing in a large room with shiny floors. People were standing around, but I couldn't make out their faces. I believe God was there. I remember asking, "Where is the demon?" and

God looked surprised to me.

It's calling me stupid. I'll fall asleep crying.

March 17th, 2017
2:00 a.m.

At times in the past years, God would periodically wake me out of my sleep to ask me a question. Used to shock me, but I grew to look forward to it. Well, red flag I awoke to a voice screaming, "Where is your king now?"

Again, I thought it was Jesus. Why? I don't know since He never screamed at me before. That's when the beating started. I was standing outside of God's temple talking to Jesus. I was screaming mad about something. He made me walk away. When I got several paces, I turned and He was swinging. In my spirit, I was beat so hard that I could feel the blows. Lucky for me, men whose faces I could not see came to pull Him off of me.

His face hated me.

Afterward, He kept trying to pull me back to Him and when I would refuse, He would beat me more. In the process of this happening, God appears to help me. HE wants to know why I didn't call HIM. Well, I was guilty because several weeks before I had cursed while speaking to HIM - I blamed HIM for allowing pedophilia. I was so mad that I carried a molested baby around on a silver platter not to mock HIM, but because I was so mad.

So I felt guilty. I figured if Isa was beating me that God was okay with that. But HE said no. Now HE told me not to speak to "Isa" anymore…but me and "I love Jesus", I would try to ignore Him, but when He pulled me to Him, I would follow, get beat on when I refused sexual advances. God would keep coming to help me, but inside I still thought I was doing something wrong.

"Jesus" said He had to clear the snakes out of His house. He was talking to me! I *thought* "**He**" was talking to me. He told me that when I died and when He saw me He was going to hurt me. His hateful was very hurtful.

Christ had never approached me sexually before, but all of a sudden He's as randy as a schoolboy and I'm the woman who is irresistible? Seemed weird. On top of that, He hit me way too hard for kissy-face to follow.

March 18th

He grabbed me by the back of my jacket and slammed me into the wall. He kicked me and punched me. He grabbed me by the head and roughly raped me orally. Afterward, he threw me in a garbage dump and peed on me. God came and told me to say the Prayer of Manasseh - that HE would protect me.

His name is Joshua. I thought he was saying Yeshua. He's tall, 6ft maybe, broad shouldered, not bad looking but very mean. His hair is kinda wild. His eyes are wild.

Why did you think that was Jesus?

I thought in all the centuries that have come and gone and all that He's been through that maybe He would be a little…odd. Never acted crazy beforebut...I remember asking Him to please not hit me in the stomach. He didn't.

March 21st

God asked me if I know the prayer again.

The obscenities are not as vicious.

Some weeks ago I bickered with the devil. I hollered, called him a girl, told him not to be standing near me on Judgment Day, said I would bring him some pink panties and ribbons for his hair. Never thought of it again.

After that, some days I would hear that I had embarrassed...someone - that I had a big mouth - which I do. I thought it was correction from the Lord. Now I understand that he was embarrassed. Why any comments I make would embarrass this sucka, I don't know, but I guess he's upset about that.

March 22nd

A short time ago I was in the tub and I felt eyes watching me while I had my adult private time - eyes looking at me down there - but I blew it off as nothing.

He's been smelling me. He tells me what I smell like - my private areas - degrades me. He sniffs my clothes. He said he was a roach that crawled out of my pocket and searched my body while I was sleeping.

March 26th

God asked me if I know the prayer.

I was lying in bed and felt a rush of something akin to fear – something less than terror. I grabbed my pistol and prayed. Of course, help came and told me to quiet – the Lord telling me to calm down. I hear a voice say, "the Jew's" hissing (me? Ok).

God was sitting over me but still he stood in the dark hallway outside my bedroom door. From the crack beneath the door, I watched a shadow move and stand outside the door. I was afraid because I could feel how badly he wanted to come in the room – like a rage that would've snapped if I provoked it. The Lord was also there. The only way to put the feeling into words is an intangible evil.

He called us a bunch of pussies. When he left, the Lord told me to lie down (go to sleep).

In my head, I could see the devil running around the living room floor in a circle. To me, he was tall and lanky. He has hooves - legs like a horse - sometimes 4, sometimes 2. The hair on his body is thin - bottom body. His upper body is similar to a man's, but the bones around his chest (hairless) and ribcage protrude like he's malnourished. That's how he was outside my bedroom.

March 29th

I told him to repent but the Lord says not to feel sorry for him.

To be clear, when one asks why God allowed me to go through these things, I will say that it is something that I want to do and I told God that.

It's not that I want it, but if the weirdo wants to continue bothering me then I will write it down. God does not allow him to touch me physically though I can feel the touching as if it's physical.

My experience will not be wasted. I won't be ran off by a weirdo. I am writing this memoir for others to read so they know what to do if they're ever in the same situation, and I pray that this memoir reaches the eyes of those who don't say anything because they don't want people to think they're CRAZY! And especially to females who have been molested by the devil willingly or unwillingly, you have to pray.

I'm counting the days.

He's talking about my hair, my teeth - my body.

Small penis, God says.

March 30th

I had a vision of him screwing me while purposefully looking me in my face because he knew it would disgust me. He is repulsive. I am sick to my stomach.

God says HE would never show me what he had in his mind to do to me.

March 31st

"God is not there where you can reach out and touch HIM…"

Jesus told me he (the devil) likes the boys (wink).

Which there's nothing wrong with that, but the statement agitated him. Now that I think about it, I've been hearing "nappy headed nigga" for about 4 years now. I thought it was just something negative that sometimes popped into my head.

Jesus told me to watch my surroundings.

April 1st

"Spiritual maturity? Who?"

Still stalking me. Still spitting, screaming, raging obscenities at God and me. Always makes references to Christ. Jealous?

Got another good laugh. He said, "Tell this hole to get a job."

He's obsessed with Isa.

Broke down in the shower. Got dizzy and laid on the floor of the tub crying and praying. I don't know what I thought was in the shower with me, but it was trying to kiss me. Still afraid to talk to Jesus because I don't know who's responding sometimes.

I don't like being naked.

April 2nd

I write this note as I lay in bed and I hear screaming - my voice screaming, "I hate you" to God - screaming like a demented fiend. He's imitated my voice.

I can hear my godson saying my name, but he's not here with me.

For weeks, he's been calling me a whore and a liar.

I've finally realized he's a hypocrite. I'm so slow. He keeps telling me to watch what I say. Still asking me questions and trying to expose me in some kind of wrong.

Sometimes I tell myself I'm crazy. I tried that today and while I was driving, on the radio popped up a sermon about Job and how Satan told God that he was walking to and fro on the earth, then somewhere else a friend talked of a pregnant whore (I planned on having a baby this year, but God called me), walk in the house and TV is playing comedy and for the first time ever I hear comedy about the devil. These things all happened in a two hour span.

    I dreamed once that I was standing in a crowd of people. We were on the street and everything was gray – gray buildings, gray streets, people moving in a blur, some walking, some running around and there was a lion in the crowd. When it saw me, it came straight for me. I thought it would bite me, but when it got right close, it turned and walked away.

    God said, "Why didn't you attack her?"

    I didn't understand then what HE meant, but now I realize that I wasn't attacked because God *was* with me.

9:00 pm

Could one being be so wicked? Powers and principalities? I don't know what that is. Is he just a dark ball of energy - a culmination of all the evil that ever happened in the world that feeds and lives on hapless souls?

11:10 pm

God's waiting for me to scream for him to get off of me.

That's comforting.

April 3rd
9:08 am

He's bringing up an insult that was made by a person from my past that badly hurt me (back then).

Told me that I don't have any faith. My heart gave a panicked jump but a second later I calmed. It's not true. Just part of the exposure process.

He wants me to know how good some females are at cunnilingus. These messages are meant to expose bad things in my heart to God though God knows what's in our hearts.

He (the devil) will accuse you.

It's crying because I'm soft-hearted – trying to play on me. Says that God let's me do whatever I want. There was a time where I knew the smell of them – or thought I did. It's an odor that's hard to describe. That's how I used to know that one of them was around – or at least I thought I did.

It says, "Angel don't want no thrills. Bet if her ass was hot enough and I was in there..."

Also, I'm a slut.

"Who do you love most - God or Jesus?" it asks.

Why I wonder?

It wants to know why I always ask for instruction instead of doing what I want or think is right?

As I prayed, it asked if I was praying to God or him. So if one is being haunted and prays, it thinks you're praying to show him (the demon) that you're praying.

8:00 pm

So he's quiet all the two hours of my business law class then soon as I walk to my car, "Slut!" – this, that. So I ask this sucka what he done made, created, caused to grow – something. Response? Nothing.

Why? Because his sorry behind is holding on just like the rest of us. He ain't nothing, ain't did nothing, the knowledge he got started with God but his dirty lips steady flapping. Dumb, disrespectful dog.

If I call God, his sorry butt be running. This is the bump in the night? So basically, he's no better than the common thugs and murderers running the street.

Ok.

He said, "I can make fire."

I was putting out a cigarette and the flames sparked. I say, "Tada, there's fire that **I** made."

He says, "I can make fire out of my nose."

I said, "Cause God made you that way. Just like I can make a baby or grow a plant."

He said, "Well, if God says..."

God says, "Well, answer her."

He wants me to accuse God. So even though God has the eagle eye, I'm still exposed. So do I blame God for something, I ask myself? I don't think so.

Then he said, "Well, HE killed Christ on the cross."

I say, "I don't know because it was a sacrifice made that I needed, but at the same time po'baby." (meaning Christ)

So he says, "They stuck Him through His stomach."

I said, "Well, why didn't you stop it - say, 'no God, don't do this - we'll find another way. This is wrong.' Why didn't you sacrifice yourself?"

He's still calling me nigras.

He's doing the crybaby voice, "You don't have any respect for me."

~ He says I'll visit him everyday. ~ Maybe he's going to jail.

Note: In editing this memoir on 5/11/2017, the above highlighted statement finally made sense.

"If Isa told you something, would you tell me?"

"Of course I would," I say. "But you know I'm a liar just like you."
(Just today I sent a $12 package out as media mail for $4)

I say to myself, "I wonder if he's ever sorry."

This sucka say, "For wanting to put it in your booty? No."

I'm about to stop talking to him.

Hours later…

Me? Irritated.

This sucka always goes for an orifice. I remember asking God to not let him touch me and even though there's no physical touching, it's still terrible in your spirit. He is terrible.

I know there's a female or man even who will pick up this memoir and recognize what I'm saying, someone who relates. He may bother me until I die, but I vow to write it all down. He will not dominate me. This memoir will help someone. Please pray.

Like make some furniture move around, make some crap fly across the room. But this pervaceous-pervyness gets on my damn nerves.

Why do I feel like I'm bothering God

by calling HIM? Because I'm embarrassed to call HIM every five minutes because the devil is being nasty. But it's my fault for talking to him. I'm queasy, shaky, want to go to the sunken place for an hour. After I say "sunken place", he laughs and God gives me half a second wind.

He says, "If you give me a pound of flesh, I can make another."

God tells me to ask where the pound of flesh comes from. I don't answer, so God holds out his hand.

"Another Me?" I say

It says, "Two."

"Ah!" I say.

And at the same time it says, "Yesss."

God told me weeks ago that my spirit

would be corrupted.

One of the reasons he doesn't like Christ is because he thinks He eats up any and everything God hands Him with awe-filled eyes. A suck-up basically - that Jesus will let HIM do anything HE wants to Him.

I say, "What can Jesus do?"

He says, "He wants it. That's the problem."

God says that the devil thinks that HE and Christ are whispering about him, but they're only talking about us.

All I can say is he tries too hard. I feel very, very sad for what he is and the feeling he brings - dread and misery. I started to say that when I try to be unbiased that I feel sorry for him, but God grabbed my arm in a death grip. When I say "death", I mean that's a path that leads to death - even for me. If one thinks about every bad thing that the devil had a hand in and so much so that God won't grant him forgiveness or repentance -

God just turned HIS face. And that, for some reason, makes me sad.

He says, "Because God won't forgive me, I want to kick you. God better sleep with one eye open."

Aye carumba!

Jesus says, "I'll be woke."

God says there's nowhere HE can't go and HE's the boss.

This all is happening while I'm folding laundry. By the way, an entire sleeve has been torn off an old nightgown at the shoulder. Maybe the dryer did it. The arm was a little ripped anyway. I'm going to blow it off as paranoia even though I'm creeped out.

Devil says, "There's people that would run to smell that gown for me."

God says, "Very little of what he says is directed at you. It's all mostly for MY benefit. In fact, very little of it is about you."

But he didn't create those "running-to-smell" people either. He says it goes both ways. I guess he's saying that if they were God's then they wouldn't be chasing *him*. I am one of those people who believe that informed adults should be free to choose their own consequences.

God says, "If you don't like how God works, WHAT YOU GONE DO?"

I say, "What is God doing that's so wrong?"

Some people are upset because of

suffering. I will admit that I have complained. I don't know. I wouldn't say that I don't feel upset sometimes - that I don't have questions - but at the end of the day, I'm on my knees. I just don't care what HE does or doesn't do. I don't know. What can you do?

And I'm taken to task for having felt sorry for him.

April 4th
2:00 a.m.

More sexually degrading comments. He told me to watch where I am all the time.

I spoke with the Lord - and yes, I know it was Him.

"For thou art not a God that hath pleasure in wickedness: neither shall evil dwell with thee."

The devil wants to know why he is allowed to persist?

Every time I doze, he pulls at my spirit - tries to drag it toward him. I've felt this feeling before in the past. The best way I can describe it is a heavy feeling - like being weighed down.

If he tricks me, I'm going to trick him back. He's mad at this book.

The devil is funny - he says funny

things. He ain't but a piece of crap, but he's humorous at times. Let me be very clear that God does not like when I laugh at his jokes - wants me to say why I'm amused in light of the fact that he tries to molest me.

I'm just not scared because God is there.

I asked God if HE talks to him. HE said that HE's allergic to him, but yes.

God doesn't like the smell on earth.

I saw him today. I was sitting in the computer lab tripping.

God says to me, "Don't panic. It's okay."

So me, "Whatever." *shrug*

So Satan says, "I'm looking you right in the face."

Me? "Whatever." I never doubted that his spirit moves around.

I look up and sure enough he's sitting right in my face - right across from me at another computer. The same face I've been seeing in my mind - damn near. A very pale man in his fifties with extremely yellow teeth and a disruptive disposition. Puckered flesh around the mouth. Thin, salt and pepper hair, weathered skin, about 5'7, 150 lbs. Wore glasses, regularly dressed - not unkempt but not neat. Pads of paper are in his jacket pocket and when he knows that I'm looking, he raises his head, chin back so that I can see his face staring at me, lowered lids. His eyes were brown, feral. I stare at him for several seconds, but he won't look me in the eye.

I ask God, "Is that him?"

Silence.

So me, "Yeah, that's his sorry butt."

My first thought is, that's okay cause I'll shoot him in the face.

He moves a seat over and says loudly in a lab where people are concentrating, "JESUS CHRIST!"

So I say, "Thank you, Jesus."

He's all huffy-puffy (irritated because I was not impressed and God was next to me smiling) and paces around, leaves out the lab, comes back. I tell him to pray. He leaves out. So I close out my program and leave.

He's sitting in the hallway outside the lab. He wants me to know how glad I should be that my Father was there.

One time when an image of him conjured, he was very dark-skinned with goldish-brown hair. The pale image is most prevalent and today finally seen in physical form. Very unsuspecting looking fellow.

10:32 p.m.

I forgot my prayer. He's mocking me and I can't remember and I panicked because the demon is stalking me. I panicked and an uncontrollable trembling has come over me but I keep praying.

"By reserving evil for me…lower parts of the earth…"

I don't want to be no animal.

I saw myself slamming my bedroom door on the devil. When I leaned against it to keep him out, a bright light shown all around the seams of the door. I hoped it was God but I thought that maybe the devil was trying to trick me, so I ran up the wall and hid in the corner. I saw myself with a dark shadow behind me. When I moved, it moved with me; where I sat, it crawled behind me.

The devil is very sensitive about what I write.

Isa stood at the top of stairs of a grated walkway and pointed down the stairs to a large black pool that was filled with what looked like vomit. I think a man was inside, but I turned my hack because I didn't want to look.

Then I was swinging on a swing suspended from nothing. The devil was near, but I wasn't worried until suddenly one of the swing's chains snapped. I was afraid but God reached in and grabbed me by my hand and pulled me out. When I looked down again, the demon was hanging from the broken chain. Below was all black

- a tunnel. Earth was at the bottom of a well.

God bet me that HE could carry me on HIS back without turning about and the devil wouldn't touch me. I can't imagine how afraid a person may be if they don't have help from God.

God has called him a thief.

I'm hearing that he's been castrated which makes me ask how he's raping. Maybe it's a mind thing?

Jesus told me to remember that he is a sneak;

"Any way that a sneak can be snuck he will sneak you. He is going to see how close he can get to you, but don't worry because God is as quick as lightning."

The Lord says he is treacherous.

From what I hear, he's swinging at air

if you have faith. God is a hedge so to speak and he is an unclean spirit.

I say that he tears down what he didn't create. But he goes round and round - curses, threats of violence, sexual vulgarity, accusations, harassment. Never changes - or will it? Once I get over the mental part, does he have to move on to physical contact? Because he is a sneak, what's next?

11:18 pm

Right now he's charging me with my crimes. There's a new sheriff in town, people.

ACCOUNT #2
Date: 4/19/17
Black female, 33 years

    I've always believed in God. I dreamed once of a white light that was full of energy and felt so good.

    I said, "If it's You, touch my hand", and He did.

    A demon bothers me. Because of my relationship with God, he would beat on me, drag me around, etc. I was scared. I would call for God.

    One time, I tricked him and acted like I was attracted to him so he would leave me alone. He came back next time in the form of my husband. In the dream, I thought maybe it wasn't my husband - but it looked like him. His penis was weird like bent and crooked and I pointed it out to him and he straightened it out.

    I said to him, "You kinda don't seem

like my husband." His eyes were weird.

After sex, he said, "You're right. I'm not your husband."

I just had a baby. I sometimes look at my baby and hope… the next time he came back, I told him no. It seemed like there was a shield around me.

After that, he would come back. I couldn't sleep because I don't want him in my dreams. My bedroom is the only one on the 2nd floor. I would hear him coming up the stairs and I would think, here come this (expletive).

I would ask, "What are you doing here? What do you want?"

He came back again and pointed in my face so I bit his finger off. It grew back with a long nail attached to it. He poked me all over my body. When he poked me in my stomach, it hurt so bad that I woke up.

My stomach was bleeding.

I saw that demon once before - this same skinny demon standing years ago at the end of my bed. I called a friend to come and be with me because I was scared. He said that in my sleep, I was shaking and hyperventilating.

When I fall asleep, if I see darkness I know the demons are coming. One demon I fought had electricity for hands.

Me and my husband started having problems. It was like this dark object was trying to attach itself to both of us - like whatever was on me was trying to find something else to jump on because it couldn't stay on me. At that time it was like a negative energy surrounded us.

Me and my sister had the same dream once of a demon chasing us. She was running and scared of him. I was running behind it.

About a month ago, my kids told me there was something in the house. Sometime later I was home alone. I was applying cosmetics and I heard someone in the house. I distinctly heard a door close and someone walk through the house. I thought it was my husband so I called out for him, but no answer, so I went looking.

I go in the basement; come back upstairs. I look all over even moving the fridge. Something hits me on the butt but I don't see anything. I move the fridge again and out of my peripheral someone walks through the living room right past me.

I have a relationship with God. When you know better, you have to do better. Those who continue to succumb are weak in temptation or weak in God.

Because the Lord loves me.

April 5th

He says I'll visit him everyday. Maybe he's going to jail. – April 3rd, 2017 note

So I was thinking that people who have killed people, have robbed, prostitutes, thieves - he tells them what kills their confidence or tempts their baser urges by suggestion and deception. Because he can't be responsible for everything, can he? We do have free will. We know the difference between right and wrong.

I can recall that after committing an intentional sin not wanting to talk to God. Maybe out of guilt or feeling that a prayer wouldn't be answered because I had done something wrong and God was probably angry with me. So when I didn't seek God, I had no guidance, and until I moved forward to reconcile, there was that in between space that I remember as a raw, wide open feeling.

It was guilt.

Sinners still talk to God though they feel they're damned but haven't been yet judged.

I am resilient. I can adapt to anything after the initial sting, but I could not get used to the raw feeling. Some people can and I guess some don't care either way.

So I say I'm an advocate so to speak. I am writing this for the next person who has been or is being attacked. If you don't have a relationship with God, you'd better get one.

People will say I'm crazy. I don't care though. If you don't seek a relationship with God, you're vulnerable and that's the bottom line.

He says, "They did not get away?"

(meaning the rape victims). "Why didn't the Lord help them the way HE helped you?"

So I asked the LORD ALMIGHTY and HE told me to get it all down.

"If you want to live in iniquity you reap the fruit of your labor."

It's been pretty quiet today, which is good because it (the devil) makes me tired.

I asked why he never mentions love; has he ever loved anything?

He says, "No."

But God said he loved HIM.

He says, "It's because God let someone else run the kingdom."

So I ask God, "He loved you or loves you?"

God said, "It doesn't matter because

we're done."

I think I'm crazy as hell.

It's the triggers that he uses to manipulate people. Small things that agitate you to get you to react - to become angry - and then it's like a domino effect. You snap on somebody or become preoccupied and other aspects and people in your life are affected which causes them to have a reaction which they **act** on - chain reaction. Hopefully, a calm person is somewhere along the chain because a thoughtful person will reflect and regroup thus releasing the negative emotion without acting on and dispensing it into the air and onto one or more other people.

So I'm standing washing dishes and I'm thinking, man, I'm probably crazy. So God turns and shows me lifting my legs in the shower.

That's so embarrassing.

He says that I can have my repentance. I have about 90 days to go.

So I say, "Wow, with this whole mind trip thing, what if I don't know when the Lord is talking to me?"

It says to God, "See, she doesn't even know."

I guess he's defending me? Gotta watch out for this...It. He's telling me to stop worrying about what others think of me; that I tear myself down; that he's got my back.

God says HE does not like that we think HE will cut us down in cold blood.

Why do we think that? Is it guilt?

HE also says that HE understands that

not everyone wants to do HIS will. Just like those that refuse to bow to Satan, there's those that refuse HIM.

The devil raised his hand.

But God says that HE's looking to fill a perfect kingdom. I wonder does that mean those who don't fit will fall by the wayside.

God says it means, "Are you going to complain every time I ask you to do or not do something? Because that signals to ME lack of respect (HE waves a dismissive hand) because you can go on about your business, but don't come running to ME when things don't go right. I AM GOD. How many times do I have to say it?"

So I say, "Well, God, what about the people who believe yet get hurt?"

HE points a finger at me and tells me, "Don't be so quick to accuse." And tells me the same thing HE always tell me - and no matter how you want to look at it, it's true -

That is:

"If it's known within society that bad things are going on, why has not the government made everyone open their doors? Illegal search is a manmade excuse. Why aren't you busting down these doors? Because a piece of paper ensures a murderers' rights? No one should be uncomfortable with opening their doors for search. I gave you the whole earth. What's the problem? You wanted your society - now you have it."

I say that God is too easy - too good - but HE says HE wants respect, not trembling fear.

The devil asked me if I was really going to put this book out; if I was really going to put it on the internet for the whole world to see; that people are going to call me crazy. He wants you all to know how he feels about it (that's what he said).

Yes, I am. It'll be the last thing I do.

God is amused - says he has a good jealousy with me.

The devil says, "Yes, because you get to behold all that glory being a slut."

So I said, "Well, what about you and what you do?"

He says, "And I'm still here."

God is holding him away from me.

I feel so small right now.
The devil says that he hates Isa.

Jesus told me that when I see it, don't panic. He's going to try to get closer and closer.

April 6th

It's my birthday.

First they pour liquid fire over his head. Christ whistled nonchalantly. They took off his vest to expose the tender areas. I didn't want to look him in the eyes, so I wouldn't feel sorry for him. They turned me around and made me look. He carries angry souls on his back inside a black mist. Now he's weak. He is Misery.

HE says one day HE'll have nothing of him but the vest.

What is a deity?

Dogs have heightened senses. Birds fly. We speak and think. Our skin breathes and lasts for decades. We have a brain. God made us all.

The good book says HIS thoughts are

not like ours. One day for HIM is like a thousand years. We don't know what HE is because we've never seen HIM. Sometimes HE's referred to as "terrible" though I've never seen it. Common sense dictates that one wouldn't create something that could hurt him/her. So if we look at all that God has created - a sun that burns, HE controls thunder and fire. HE's ancient - very old. Ezekiel described a glorious likeness of a man. In the Apocryphal, Enoch described a terrible burning face.

What is a deity? And since there's only the One, what is HE? ☺

So when you think about it, all of creation is not a puppet, because we have free will, but aren't we more like robots, living things HE created of all kinds, crawling things and two-legged creatures called "human" that start out as infants and grow into old people so HE can watch us grow and change. We think too much of ourselves. If HE stopped time for 24 hours, we wouldn't know. HE makes night and day. We're just life forms no better than a cow or a deer but-for the fact that HE put them under us.

If God had a secret place, how would we know? What we are so puffed up for, I don't know. Even the angels who have to have more knowledge than us could have their switch flipped just like us.

So with the accusing, it's mostly in the area of sex with Jesus - or just sex period. Always vulgar. I have weaknesses in other areas, but that's where he concentrates. Is that because sexual immorality gets beneath God's skin more than anything else? Why not threaten to bludgeon me or cut my head off? All I get is him trying to perform some sex act on me, ask me about women though I'm not a lesbian – just sexual vulgarity. Is he just a pervy fellow or what?

He's diseased. He wants to be able to approach me in a dream. Now he's trying to be my friend when I was a "bitch" two minutes ago. Maybe "bitch" is a term of endearment. He wants respect. When I close my eyes, he's standing over me at an incline. I was out earlier at the casino. I had a sensation like a hard solid thump like I was punched hard in the shoulder but with a knife. Now I see demons swinging from the cameras, dark mists interfering with the patrons, flipping chips.

He tried to fly into my mouth and nest in my stomach but God pulled him out and blocked my openings. HE told me not to say anymore "what is a deity" and how HE has to work so hard just to have a relationship with HIS own kids.

HE asked me to do this one thing for HIM. I said yes. I trust HIM.

April 7th

I have with God an obsession. That is why a whole lot of them can't crawl in me. I feel self-conscious naked. He keeps telling me to call Him "Father", but I don't feel worthy.

He's (the devil) going to keep offering me stuff though he doesn't know what I like. God showed me how he doesn't know me. He's smiling and offering me black licorice. I don't like black licorice.

He said, "You don't know which god you're talking to."

It's a decrepit dog with a bad left arm that can only attack our minds.

He says I'll visit him everyday. Maybe he's going to jail. – April 3rd, 2017 note

Feels bad to have almost been raped by a demon. Makes my stomach turn. His head is spinning around like in the movies. I'm crazy as hell.

They said, "Don't talk to him."

Dark shadow in shape of man ran behind me as I walked to the kitchen. Just happened to look over my shoulder and there it was.

April 8th

"I wanted a steel bar heavily weighted on one end..."

    Rape, rape, rape. Rape in my vagina. Rape in my butt. Same bull getting on my nerves.

<u>Prayer of Manasseh</u>

"O Lord, Almighty God of our Fathers Abraham, Isaac, and Jacob and of their righteous seed..."

Pray

"Who hast made heaven and earth with all the ornament thereof..."

Man cutting down good trees – trees with deep roots – uprooting life living within. Makes HIM feel spiteful that HE could split a mountain in two just by looking at it.

"Who hast bound the sea by the word of thy commandment..."

Oil and trash dumped in rivers and oceans

"Who has shut up the deep and sealed it by thy terrible and glorious name…"

Thick, deep billowing clouds rising above the mountains

"Whom all men fear, and tremble before thy power…"

God passing over a valley where two men, one black one white, are having intercourse.

"For the majesty of thine glory cannot be borne, and thine angry threatening toward sinners is importable;"

God saying to man, "And you're mad at ME?"

"But thy merciful promise is unmeasurable and unsearchable;"

But God says, "That's okay. I'll forgive you."

"For thou art the most high Lord, of great compassion, longsuffering, very

merciful, and repentest of the evils of men. Thou, O Lord, according to thy great goodness hast promised repentance…"

"To you," HE says, pointing.

"... and forgiveness…"

HE says, "And you." Looks like He means it.

"… to them that have sinned against thee: and of thine infinite mercies hast appointed repentance unto sinners, that they may be saved."

"See," HE says.

"Thou therefore, O Lord, that art the God of the just, hast not appointed repentance to the just, as to Abraham, and Isaac, and Jacob, which have not sinned against thee; but thou hast appointed repentance unto me that am a sinner: for I have sinned above the number of the sands of the sea."

HE says that HE's had it up to HIS

forehead...though there are some that HE enjoys.

"My transgressions, O Lord, are multiplied: my transgressions are multiplied, and I am not worthy to behold and see the height of heaven for the multitude of mine iniquities. I am bowed down..."

HE says, "Isa is bowed down. None of us have bowed that far."

"...with many iron bands, that I cannot lift up mine head, neither have any release: for I have provoked thy wrath, and done evil before thee: I did not thy will, neither kept I thy commandments: I have set up abominations, and have multiplied offences. Now therefore I bow the knee of mine heart, beseeching thee of grace. I have sinned, O Lord, I have sinned, and I acknowledge mine iniquities: wherefore, I

humbly beseech thee, forgive me, O Lord, forgive me, and destroy me not with mine iniquities. Be not angry with me for ever, by reserving evil for me; neither condemn me to the lower parts of the earth. For thou art the God, even the God of them that repent; and in me thou wilt shew all thy goodness: for thou wilt save me, that am unworthy, according to thy great mercy. Therefore I will praise thee for ever all the days of my life: for all the powers of the heavens do praise thee, and thine is the glory for ever and ever. Amen

April 9th

So I was tired when I woke up this morning. I've been taking a Benadryl at night to help me sleep and the drowsiness hadn't worn off. I had breakfast plans with a friend, but when I got back home, I took another half of a pill planning to sleep most of the day. I wake up and something is kissing me. Am I losing my damn mind? But it's my fault because I keep thinking about this stuff when Jesus is telling me to pay attention to something else.

He says I'll visit him everyday. Maybe he's going to jail. - April 3rd, 2017 note

April 10th
12:40 am

This sucka would literally act like the Lord. He'll be like wearing a similar black robe or something. Will start off saying something pleasant and when I respond in kind will insult me nicely.

Example:

Doing well today?
Me: Yes.
Whores usually are.

Fell sleep face down on the couch - a deep sleep, the kind where if I think I'm walking into a nightmare, I have to struggle to get my lids open. I was dreaming but something was on my back like a heavy weight. I remember saying, I hate you *expletive* and a tightening on my back, a shaking shadow of anger and I screamed for God - said the words because they came to mind, "Get off of me!" - and woke up. This time it wasn't sexual but more like an aggression as if I can be forced into submission.

1:00 am

HE told me, "Go lay right back down on the couch." So I'm going.

10:11 am

    I forgot him from last summer. Summer before he was bothering me while at the gas station. A bee attacked me and I said something smart. Again, the bee flew at me when I thought it was gone. He called it a Bee on Rollerblades.

    Saw him this morning while jogging, the Bumblebee on Rollerblades. A real bee but still the devil right under my arm.

    This sucka got control issues. I don't know if he has kids, but he sure act like he do. Maybe that's why God keeps reiterating that HE's the father.

"Why you not doing this, why you doing that, don't say nothing to God."

Sucka please. Jive turkey wanna lay on me, put his weight on me, try and pull me where he wants me to go to do what he wants me to do, be all in my business trying to expose me in front of God when he's a murdering, thieving, trickster. Quite a pervy fellow too if I may say so. Obsessed with Jesus' sex life. For me, that raises a brow.

8:24 pm

So I've always wondered why God offered Jesus as a sacrifice. I'm sitting here watching YouTube and HE says, "It's like the rainbow. I will never do it again."

God has to always save me because this joker steady pulling at my knickers.

April 11ᵗʰ
9:18 am

"…it's the demons that you can't see."

So this dog wakes me up this morning talking to me. Now only God usually does that, but now I have to be on guard because this sucka is around. I get a vision of a man who watches a little girl riding her bicycle the same way everyday, a black man after a little brown girl who's happy to be riding her bike. He throws something on the ground – nails or glass so she gets a flat tire and he can talk to her. I'm looking dead in his face and the man was embarrassed and moves away, but I can see what he planned on doing to her little body.

Now this (expletive) Satan – everybody knows how I feel about pedophiles.

He keeps saying, "Well, what about

God?"

He wants me to accuse and complain against God. Lil' tricky (expletive). So I get pissed. Of course, my favorite word for him is used at least 50 times because he is a lil' (expletive).

"You done been in my bathroom, in my bedroom, know what my butt smell like, all in my face trying to smell my breath, tried to screw me while acting like Jesus, done disrespected God in my face to HIS face, even making sexually immoral references to HIM while calling HIM names…"

So again, I want to fight this (expletive), but God keeps us separated cause he's a lil' cheating (expletive).

Long story short, I'm in a room with his ugly (expletive) and there's a door, so I open it, and there's all these dark mists floating around. This (expletive) wants me to know that if he wasn't locked in this room we would have a problem, but that's not true cause his ass is too slow. So God comes and tosses his stanky acting (expletive) in the room and holds on to me and tells me to look down. So I do and it's all darkness.

HE says it goes so deep and there's so many souls down there. I ask why they don't fight since they're all so evil. Because they're all evil is the answer - what's the point?

This (expletive) adds, "Because a house divided cannot stand."

So again he's mocking me for sassing the God because he knows it burns me. That's fine. I'll say the lil' (expletive) is right. But at the same time, I feel like if I'm upset and I'm talking to God his punk (expletive) shouldn't be ear-hustling all in my business. God knows how to correct me - has done so before - and is extremely efficient, hits the aim dead on. Trust me.

I'm tired of this ugly…

9:40 p.m.

So now that I think about it, I remember that every time I try to draw close to God, I'm bothered by this demeaning or violent activity. But he called me a bitch even when I was bad but never came close, or I never noticed because I was doing the wrong things. When I moved toward repentance, he tried to snatch me off the couch and we fought in the living room until I prayed.

When I fell all the way for God, we stayed in communication and HE coddled me. Next thing I know, my best friend is raped, my brother dies in ruin, and I do something so stupid that I wouldn't tell nobody but Jesus (comeuppance but stung all the same). In one year's time!

What came with those events? A demeaning voice full of put downs that co-mingled with the divine voice which directed me. Guilt. And a trickster. I fell for it.

But never sexual before except a dream I had of watching him rape a woman a long, long time ago. Things have definitely changed. Just like now knowing where the put downs are actually coming from, I'm like "I'm dying and this (expletive) is still going everyday a month later". What that tells me is he's trying to keep me from a great future. Telling me not to pray. He's trying too hard. Getting on my damn nerves too. Sometimes I want to fight him, but God says he'll only make me tired.

11:19 p.m.

Take a Benadryl, lay down to listen to the Letter of Jeremiah on YouTube. I close my eyes and see me lying naked over his lap facedown. Some lady is saying, "Oh no, she doesn't know what that means."

He's got horns like a ram. Chest like a man - bones protruding. The body of a horse. Hooved hands. He's mad but he doesn't know what to do. Jesus said they tricked him. Time will show it as always. Clarity comes when you're not looking for it. I was thinking maybe they didn't trick him - just playing his mind. Kind of a trick within a trick.

The dog says, "You know me, I'll just keep ticking" - anything to shake his fist at God, who's looking at him right now like HE can't stand him with the "I can't stand you" face.

He (the devil) says, "I don't care."

God told me to make sure I get that.

It says, pointing. "Look at my face."

I guess that facial expression means it's serious about not caring.

April 12th
12:47 pm

Jesus says to stop calling Him God. There's only one God - HE's got HIS own body, HE is who you put your trust in, that even He, Himself, is guided by God, He doesn't advise God nor does HE need His advice. God has HIS own spirit; did not die on the cross; could not be ran through by a man with a knife, sword, stick, or imagination - the instrument of death would not be able to hold HIM. HE is too holy and too strong to be struck down for or by man. God was never a man. Jesus would like to be a separate entity from God. Thank you for your prayers, praise God. He is always happy to help lead you on the path toward God.

Example: Richie behaves just like his dad.

Jesus has His Father in Him. He is not God.

When I think about it - that he watched me, tried to climb his stinking carcass in my bed, tried to be seductive and aggressive when he's a repulsion - it burns me. There's a heat in my chest, but I'm not gonna cry because I believe - know that he's going to get what's coming to him.

Then always asks me about God. No. What did you do? Then to come back every single day and check me - try to control me. I want to kill this bitch.

ACCOUNT #3
April 21st, 2017
Black female, 34 years

Q: So you know that if you hear that bad voice condemning you, that's not God?

A: I asked God a question and He answered me.

Q: But you do believe in God?

A: Yes. But how were we created? All I know is, I believe in God.

Q: What about Christ? Genesis. In the beginning, God created heaven and earth. Christ is not God. You know?

A: But how do we know? I believe in the Son, Christ. I don't believe in Messiah. I don't believe on Jehovah Witnesses and that. I'm Baptist. We don't know where HE came from and where He came from. I don't like when people tell me what to believe. You believe what you believe; I'll believe what I believe.

Q: God created Christ too.

A: But how do we know?

Q: I remember you telling me you had dreams about the devil. Any recent?

A: I've had some recently about God. I was talking to Him in my sleep.

Q: Do you want to tell me about them?

A: No.

Q: No dreams about the devil?

A: No, he knows now…

Q: Tell me again about the devil dreams.

A: My dreams about demons usually follow from the use of alcohol, which makes me vulnerable. One particular time, I remember I laid down and closed my eyes. When I opened them, the room was split – one side was in dark shadows, the other side was bright and the people looked like they were in the choir. They didn't move and didn't say anything, but their eyes were big and round and they stared at me as if pleading.

I wondered why they didn't say anything. From the dark side of the room I couldn't see anyone, but I heard voices saying, "This is the true religion. He's the real God."

Still the people on the bright side of the room didn't say anything but just stared at me as if hoping I made the right decision. On the dark side of the room, a hand reached for me. He didn't show himself, but there was a dark shadow hand.

To those on the bright side of the room I said, "Well, y'all aren't saying anything", so I lifted my foot to move to the dark side of the room and my heart suddenly felt pinched and I said, "No!"

He got mad then and I remember him just kicking me in the chest. I describe it as a Bruce Lee kick.

Q: In your dream, did it hurt?

A: In my dream, yes. I fought though. I couldn't beat him and when I got tired God jumped in.

Q: Any others?

A: I had a lot of dreams with demons. Once after drinking with a neighbor, I dreamed that a demon that looked like the one from the Exorcist was chasing me. I was very afraid and I was running. Another person was running behind the demon.

As I ran, it felt as if my feet were sinking in sand. When I was very tired, God lifted me up. I awoke with my sister standing over me. She said she woke me because I was shaking. She said she came downstairs because she heard feet running in the living room. She thought it was the kids but found that they weren't home.

When I told her my dream, we were both surprised to learn that we were in a dream together. She was chasing the demon because she knew if she was scared, it would beat her. She knew she had God.

Q: I remember another you were telling me –

A: Wait. Hold on. This is bad news.

Q: What is it?

A: I'll call you back.

- After taking this account, God told me to know that HE's my father and I'd better start telling people. I don't feel worthy for that.

A voice said, "She's trying to get on the ground floor."

This sucka sneering in my face cause I'm sitting on some floor with my book.

I say, "I rebuke you Satan in the name

of the Father (never used "rebuke" in a sentence. Don't know where that came from) cause I just talked to HIM and HE told me HE's my Father, weirdo."

So this sucka say, "I ain't scared of you, nigga."

He's afraid of the choir - whatever that means.

I say, "So what. You better hope I can't find another account because I hope it's 20 pages."

So he's sitting with my bracelet on and my wig and rocking back and forth crying. I guess he's "playing" me.

I ask the Lord, "Can I put it in the book?"

He says, "If you want, but I don't see it."

He's funny sometimes. He prays for me too.

April 13th

I'm tired of this pervert.

12:00 p.m.

So we watch infiltration in our kids' schools. The Satanic Church is attempting after school programs in our schools. The Satanic Church? One sits right here in Detroit. If the devil keeps trying me, I'm gonna talk to one of his members up close.

If you allow yourself to be guided by a liar and a trickster than you must be one as well.

People fall down and worship a being that can't give them squat. He can offer riches that he murdered, thieved or manipulated for…ah, I can do all those things on my own and probably still have a better chance at repentance than if I allow a no-account, perverted being to dominate my existence.

So since one can maim and rob on their own, what exactly is it that this sucka does? He's not trustworthy and will lie to his own followers.

If I turn the table, I deal with God because HE enriches my spirit. Of course, HE blesses me with things, but HE's my solid dude. Maybe people deal with the devil to help them be more corrupt in spirit, but after a while when do you say, "Got It" and put panties on this sucka because he's weak as hell? Yes, I'm pissed at the audacity.

Christ was 40 days in the desert starving and all he had to offer Him was riches. Somebody save me. Offer Him a hamburger, a glass of ice water. You're offering pennies in exchange for diamonds and gold.

Then they lie and say, "Oh, we don't worship the devil."

And I quote High Priest Peter Gilmore stating:

"My real feeling is that anybody who believes in supernatural entities on some level is insane. Whether they believe in the Devil or God, they are abdicating reason."

And then I see:

"Church members may also participate in a system of magic which LaVey defined as "*greater and lesser magic*". Greater magic is a form of *ritual* practice and is meant as *psychodramatic catharsis* to focus one's emotional energy for a specific purpose; lesser magic is the practice of **manipulation** by means of applied psychology and **glamour** (or **"wile and guile"**) to bend an individual or situation

<u>to one's will</u>."

So basically, Lies and Trickery. Sounds like the devil to me. According to them, Satan is Hebrew for "adversary" or "opposer". Why Hebrew? Why not use "adversary" in Russian, Mandarin, or Afrikaan? Then there's the statute and the carnality. We have enough promiscuity on earth without his help.

By the way, think about that. Sex with one person (orally or genital-to-genital) means sleeping with every person that person ever slept with.

Ladies and Gentlemen, waiting on God for a spouse? I'll tell my readers like Jesus told me: "Keep your legs closed".

I took that to mean this: Why would HE give away one of HIS best for a spouse to another human being who sleeps around? I know, ladies. Every man you sleep with –

well, you had the feeling that he was the one. It didn't work out, cry a tear in a bucket and move on to the next one.

Jesus says, "Keep your legs closed".

For those who wait patiently, you'll get what you ask for.
Gentlemen, just having a little fun. It's okay to walk away from her because she was a slut? If you sleep with her, what does that make you?
Jesus says, "Keep your legs closed".

Anyway, now we've all heard the same stories about God and the Bible. There's a lot of religions to choose from. Choose what's best for you, what you're comfortable dealing with the consequences of because God isn't puny. I say, be an atheist and refrain from evil so when your number comes up…hey, at least you're not evil and all you missed out on is the wondrous personality of God.

Question: Why would God allow the devil to frustrate His purpose?

God says to "challenge HIM". If we all do right, HE will make everything alright.

What about those that won't do right?

To my, "what is a deity?" He is God. When one of us falls off, his brother is supposed to pick him up.
"Why do you lock rapists in tall houses only to free them years later? Send them to ME and I'll know whether to uplift or smash them. How many starving children could be fed with the money used to house them? When policeman and doctors ask, 'Why?' I say, 'Be strong, blot out the bad when you see it because you are light.' And they get upset at ME because they need to hear ME say the words. But they are

only so strong. When their hearts give out, they will have their reward. Your world picks and chooses who the law kills. I AM GOD."

God does not think as men.

"Everything needed for a human being to survive is on earth. Who's in charge?"

The devil will try to:

Coerce. Threaten. Attempt to sexually attract you by trying to figure out what turns you on, he will try to disgust you with what terrifies you, either expose what he thinks makes you look guilty before a God that sees down to the marrow. He's arrogant, accuses God.

April 14th
12:23 a.m.

Trying to block me from communicating with God and thinks he's blinding me because I talk to Jesus rarely now – for several years talk to Him and God every day, all day – now just God because this bastard is a slippery (expletive) and I'm too paranoid.

He (the Lord) breaks in though. Then the bastard comes-a-humping. That's the pattern. Very annoying. I will stay the course as long as God helps me.

As I'm dozing, he says that he doesn't have anything to lose; that he's like the lifers – "he's done".

8:30 am

"Why do people get helped to move toward repentance, but I didn't?"

That's his question - with his lying ass.

Lord says, human beings can be damned off of one incident, but the devil has too many incidents.

I guess God feels that he's a screw up.

He says he wants Jesus to bow to him.

But I say, "That's not what God wanted."

A God example:

I have a lot of shoes that I don't wear. I wear the same shoes all the time. I have begun to sell these shoes on eBay. A few days ago, God told me to give a pair of boots to someone. We'll call them Person A. I say ok. So this made me look at other shoes and think, well, maybe Person A would also like these.

Five minutes ago, HE suggested that I

give a particular cute pair of shoes to another person. We'll call them Person B. I love Person B, but instantly I say no because she does this, that and the other, and I don't like that she does this, that, and the other (because it's very bad for her). I know this from my own experience and she knows it's bad too (and won't stop) and I don't want her wearing MY (heh) shoes while she's doing this, that, and the other (which I know she will). Seems judgmental, but I'm human.

I get the point. I understand what HE's saying. It amuses me when HE tells me something and it comes out later.

Out running. One bee again under arm. No roller blades

April 15th

He was in the lab again in an ugly flannel. Very authoritative all the time now.

I said the prayer. And I was about to have a heart attack cause HE was reading my heart. First HE said HE wanted to take me then. While I was saying the prayer, I was thinking other things. I said, I'll have strength.
God says, "You have ME."

Then I was thinking all the bad stuff about me and not feeling worthy, you know. Then God was looking at me up and down like, so I started to feel worried. I was thinking this "expletive-the devil". Then I was like, I'm not gonna give up.

HE said to me, my strength makes HIM want to challenge me. I was scared God wanted to fight me. Now my teeth are chattering and I feel a little faint. I don't have no strength. I don't know what happened.

The devil is trying to trick me. He's trying to trick me. I remember God's voice in the kitchen and it comforts me. He's trying to make me forget.

Haven't had a drink since Joshua.

10:20 p.m.

Double dong?

Isolation

The trail of everything leads to God. Paper comes from trees that were made by who? God. Eggs come from chickens who were made by who? God. If there's enough on earth for everyone, why are people starving? Who told us to sell what we can't create?

April 16th
12:22 p.m.

And with the flipping and prying me for answers - this sucka will try to expose you. Lord told me to stop talking to him. Is this sucka trying to get to know me for the set up? He goes from nasty and insulting most times to trying to be my friend, tells me I can't tell people what to believe, shut up talking to God, trying to initiate sex, ask me a thousand questions, adds scenarios so my brain can take off and he can manipulate my thinking and God has to redirect me, wants to know why I can't be an independent thinker, why do I seek guidance from God on everything, threatens violence, asks you a question which your brain automatically reworks against your will - to try and expose you to God who knows you or to play out his little fantasies.

God gives me breaks from this joker though. This muthasucka thinks he's the sheriff. Talking about I don't deserve to see all that glory when his weirdo can't even repent.

Then I sit up and feel bad about an insecurity. O boy, she's not going to church on Easter! That's me. I go to church once or twice a year, but God and the Lord are in my head ALL DAY. Now I'm feeling guilty? Why? Because of him? Girl bye.

And let's not forget the bad girl image. I'm watching my UFC Fight Night. Girls are fighting. Yay! They're on the ground on their sides - kinda spooning like. One girl has the other in a headlock choking her out.

Why am I seeing the girl that's

getting choked crying and struggling – tough girl – to no avail because the demon is choking her while screwing her?

See the thing about it is this, that girl getting screwed followed the demon, but now she wants out – mind you, tough girl – and thinks there's no help for her. But she still has repentance – you can see it in her face. So if the demon is trying to force me, who is protected by God, to not speak to God – if the demon is trying to make me feel guilty, what is he doing to that girl? So how many girls sit up all night afraid of this sucka? And he is terrible, despicably perverted, would rape and murder me, leave me lying in my own filth, disrespectful, has 1000 faces. Will try to coax you, offer you things.

God says he's misery.

He will use your own guilt against

you. He will try to fool you - in any way that you can be fooled or tricked, he will do it. Got me walking around saying "I'm talking to the God of Abraham" cause this sucka will sit on a throne and try to fool me.

God was talking. HE said, "Give them a little intuition, a little inquisitiveness…"

Because I wonder how HE made everything. So my dumb butt gone ask, "Are we assembled like by parts? Like is there a part labeled *Curiosity - Mild, Medium, High*?

So I'm editing a book and I'm thinking, "Man, I gotta get outta here and go see my mom."

This sucka gone say in the demon movie

voice (I'm not making this stuff up) "Did I tell you, you could go see your mom?"

    Who the hell he think he talking to? But that's my fault though. The Lord been telling me all day to stop talking to him, but I'm like a child – the sucka provokes me and I retort.

April 17th
12:55 a.m.

"This sucka is crazy. He remind me of that doll Chucky when he was about to be burned."

Sinning is hard work – I'll say that. I have more (things) now than I did back then.

12:55 pm

On the internet just browsing and come across this:

http://www.charismamag.com/spirit/spiritual-warfare/15889-can-you-be-raped-by-the-devil

Holy Comoly!

I have to find more.

I have a personal acquaintance that had a sexual experience with the devil. I don't know how she did it. I'm going to ask her if he's vulgar to her now. She's someone I love, but I don't know how she did it because them things is nasty. Trying to introduce a succubus (female sex demon). That's where all that lesbian talk came from (love lesbians just not one) trying to corrupt me.

And I remember this loved one telling me that it was a very intensely pleasurable experience, (maybe because she thought she was with her mate), which I'm reading over and over in my search. Just oughtta be pleasurable because one is losing their soul in the process. And humans are extremely carnal creatures.

I remember him saying that he would "wear my ass out" and I'm reading that, too, is common. As well as he TRICKS women/men into believing that he's _someone else_.

I took it as an invasion of my

privacy. A very hurtful experience. I thank God; it could've been worse. HE came and HELPED ME which *is* the POINT. Makes me wonder for people who don't feel that God would help them…maybe because at first they consented…I don't know.

This sucka is screaming, "Would they want help if now the experience isn't any more pleasurable?"

Very, very sad people are right now somewhere being violated by…something - but I won't let the experience go to waste. It was very, very hurtful to me. I am extremely, very embarrassed because of it because that thing is nasty…the feeling of it is miserable. I can't imagine if I didn't have God in my life. I'm reading that a succubus will lay beneath a man. Very disgusting.

I cannot speak from experience only to

say that they will try to see what arouses you, but I doubt that the experience with them is more pleasurable than sleeping with a human person if that human is considerate of your desires. You're better off bouncing on a fence pole. Demons seek out what you want to steal your soul by any means necessary.

My experience will not go to waste.

So like humans, as an imposter, he will start off with a congenial, friendly statement, which leads directly into an insult.

I remember when I was a little girl about five. My grandmother lived on a road called Livernois in a basement apartment. In an upstairs apartment was a family - a man and his wife and their little girl who was about my age. We used to play together. One day I was at her house and we were playing.

I don't know how we got on the subject, but I remember her telling me that she believed in the devil and asking me who I believed in. I remember her mother sitting close by and me having the sensation that she was listening to our conversation, which was awkward feeling but okay with me, I guess. Whenever I think of the mother, I remember her in all black.

The girl had black hair. I don't know if she was Caucasian or Hispanic maybe, but I knew she was not black like me. I knew that.

I said to her, "I believe in both."

As an adult, that always bothered me - that I split my allegiance. I was just a little girl but I don't know why I said that. Maybe because I wanted to be friends. I believed in God, my mother taught me, but I wanted to get along. I don't know.

And, of course, this…
Genesis 6:4 - 6
"**There were giants in the earth in those days; and also after that, when the sons of God came in unto the daughters of men, and they bare *children* to them, the same *became* mighty men which *were* of old, men of renown.**
And GOD saw that the wickedness of man *was* great in the earth, and *that* every imagination of the thoughts of his heart *was* only evil continually.
And it repented the LORD that he had made man on the earth, and it grieved him at

his heart."

I wonder how HE felt after making Eden. Was HE happy? How kind HE was to think to give Adam a mate. But alas, we can't make it to the second book of the bible before all hell breaks loose - the third chapter and this sucka is already trying to ruin everything. And that's just how he is too - like an attachment, an annoyance that brings misery.

Genesis 3

"Now the serpent was more subtil than any beast of the field which the LORD God had made. And he said unto the woman, Yea, hath God said, Ye shall not eat of every tree of the garden?

And the woman said unto the serpent, We may eat of the fruit of the trees of the garden

But of the fruit of the tree which *is* in the midst of the garden, God hath said, Ye shall not eat of it, neither shall ye touch it, lest ye die.

And the serpent said unto the woman, Ye shall not surely die:

For God doth know that in the day ye eat thereof, then your eyes shall be opened, and ye shall be as gods, knowing good and evil."

And. She. Fell. For. It.

Genesis 3:3

"And the LORD God said unto the woman, What *is* this *that* though hast done? And the woman said, The serpent beguiled me, and I did eat."

Are humans dumb? Yes. Don't judge, Angel. Could've been you. I don't know what's going on.

April 19th

The first and only time I visited New Orleans was an eye opener. This was some years after the flood, but whole neighborhoods were still empty; the houses were boarded up and vacant. It was fall and nothing was really going on. We visited a blues bar, I ate this really good red cabbage at a German restaurant, I did visit Bourbon St. and bought some antique jewelry.

I can't remember if it was on Bourbon or just a street nearby, but in our sight seeing, we happened to stroll past a store for foreign gods. The first thing I thought was, "Oh my God, I wish my mother was here to see this. She would have a lot to tell me."

Well, I crossed the street. I didn't want anything to do with that, but I did gawk. To think that sitting smack dab in public is this type of merchandise for sale! Oh, ok. New Orleans does have a voodoo reputation. But me, if I don't see a thing going on - hey, whatever - out of sight, out of mind.

 So who passes me on the street but this guy wearing some teeth as a necklace. Whose teeth? I don't know. Some animal's maybe? His eyes are blank and empty - nothing. A zombie. Well kiss my (expletive) and call me Suzy. I don't get out much, but stands to reason that this dude probably thinks I look weird with all my hallelujah and cross tattoos (the ring finger of my left hand. Very proud). Because when you love God it shows on your face. God-fearing people know what I'm talking about. Just like when one sees a person with a dark soul - they just look that way in their eyes. I'll bet atheists think that we all look crazy.

7:50 pm

Second time I've heard that the devil don't like mirrors. Especially on his face. He really creeps me out.

God asked me what really was the problem. I said, he doesn't have repentance.

The devil says he's going to keep hurting God's people and that he's got pictures.

God says he doesn't deserve repentance.

April 20th
9:26 am

I'm so slow. So all this time I'm thinking that HE's saying that it's castrated (meaning the devil is castrated). No. HE's telling me to think that he's castrated so when he's bothering me with his perversion if I think he has no penis, then he doesn't. It works!

The bastard says he has hands. That's ok. There's the thing about forced penile penetration that is traumatic…thank you God!

4:35 pm

God always tells me HE's with me. More than any other time right now while I'm going through this "whatever", I have never felt this paid attention to or watched. I literally feel eyes on me.

My thoughts are different. Now I'm

chasing the devil naked {since that's how he always portrays me) but now with large spikes all over my body...I'm bloody.

He's trying to make me feel like I put God second to Jesus.

Sometimes he yells at me, "You're not supposed to associate!"

So to the sexual stuff, it's now oral after the castration. So the question I ask - because he's so DISGUSTING - is why would I do anything sexual with him? I can find any strange man walking down the street who'll willingly screw me, in a bar, at the park. Why would I defile myself with this muthasucka? I could go outside and find two men to work me over and still fare better at Judgment. On top of that, this sucka is disgusting. I resent that he has situated himself in my life.

But mostly, I miss my personal time. You never realize how much you enjoy a thing until it's gone. Calgon take me away to Personal Time Land without this weird muthasucka.

April 21st
12:31 am

So I've been noticing that he's using subliminal messages like those recordings people listen to in order to influence their thinking.

I'm lying in the living room and something smells. He was running around in here a couple weeks ago. Isa asks me if I smell it. I say yeah.

And HE wouldn't lie to me. He really is castrated. It's fake. God is not negligent.

1:15 pm

Back in the computer lab. Same man. He's quiet for at least an hour then all I hear - same as before - is him saying, "Jesus Christ! Goddamnit! Shit!"

Keep in mind that, he's loud and vulgar on a college campus in a comp lab.

Seems like he really, really has a problem with Jesus. I don't know what happened between them but it's not healthy. The devil asks me questions about Him, always comments about Him - like he makes me wonder if he wants to be closer with Him (wink). He admires Him - no, fixates on Him. But it's kinda weird…you know, when you hate someone you call them names, threaten. He did call Him a "motherfucker" to me once. I don't know. It raises my brow. God keeps saying its jealousy.

I must say that I expected more from "The Devil". Not this. There's sex and blasphemy. Where's the murder and mayhem? I mean, I know God is watching over me, but - ok. I know he can't hurt me, but if there's sexual images why not an image of me getting my head blown off? The sex to violence ratio has been 80/20 with sex being pervertedly prevalent. Isa says he does it because it (sex stuff) hurts me.

But what I can handle does comes through.

Give me a car blowing up across from my house, a person getting hit by a car mere seconds before I step out of the way – something. A month ago the sex stuff bothered me but a month later it's just mostly irritating. He's very childish to me. I just expected more – more intellect, more…cleverness.

I mean, how old is he? Trickery should not be wholly relied on or necessary at that age. I know God again is helping me, but with what is allowed to happen, I still think there should be more than sex. Plus, he's too in a rush, on me too hard, dogging my steps. Even with physical contact restricted…obviously he's limited - I know he asked for time with me in hell without God as just another example of what I'm speaking of. What sense would that make?

He slams stuff, is agitated, arrogant, illogical. Where does this big bad rep come from? If it were me, I would watch a body and see what makes them tick. If you're consistently nice, a person feels safe and liked and will usually open up and trust, especially when they aren't expecting to be betrayed in the end. I would've started there.

I've been celibate for a long time so I thought that maybe he thought the sex stuff would entice me even though he's disgusting. He's boring. I have to get an eyeball on who actually enjoys his company.

5:18 p.m.

They don't like it when I laugh because of him.

Telling me don't talk to him.

April 22ⁿᵈ
1:19 pm

How do you know it wasn't the devil?

Lord says, "You know because he wasn't trying to do anything inappropriate."

I said, "Put his hands in my butt."

Maced a dog while jogging.

I thought the Lord was more like a preacher but He says more like a policeman. Last night, I dreamed an unmarked police car was in front of me on a freeway exit – the Lord in front of me. He was following me, but still, in front of me.

He keeps telling me not to talk to him, but I fall for taunts or invitation to confrontation.

He (the devil) won't stop with the sex stuff so I got mad and went trolling Facebook for Satan worshippers – not to demean them. I was mad but being emotional won't get me what I want, which is to see if I could take someone's account. Jesus won't let me though so I feel like I have no recourse. I would've met at a Starbucks or somewhere public. I have my pistol.

So then He reminds me of one of the Satanists I saw. Most of them look either crazy or kinda lost. But one stood out. In his face, one can see that the devil has him - something about the eyes. The Lord said they would've "made me" coming through the door. I guess I look prayerly.

God says he (the devil) would've ran to warn them. Now HE also says it's ok if I want to fight with one, but HE doesn't want me near them; that they'll find a way to worm themselves inside my car.

HIS nose is turned up.

In looking at their page, I'm

confused. Some Satanists say they don't believe in Satan as a god; that their church's name means "adversary" in Hebrew. Why not use adversary in - whatever.

Then these theistic Satanists worship Satan. So what I gather from Lucifer/Satan. Facebook page, he (the devil) isn't a god and they don't worship him, BUT THEN…he is a god, but he wants people to make their own decisions, be independent, but all "Hail him Creator of Blah". So some deny that they worship him and others are proud to say they worship him.

I do see that they think I'm crazy too and those like me (Jesus freaks). Their Facebook posts demeaning God and Jesus are there. Again, it was <u>Lucifer/Satan (period)</u>.

Our feeling toward one another is

mutual though. I don't know understand what their problem is either. I mean, I follow the Most High God. He's perfect, duh.

But as it stands, we both think that the other is full of BS.

April 23rd
9:15 a.m.

I hope no one reads this and says, "Where is God for this woman?"

I hope people remember trials that other god-fearing people had to endure. God is with me and I am not harmed beyond what I can handle. What are we, if we can't stand up for our God the way He does for us?

The devil is a liar.

2:30 pm

My brother just called to ask if I was okay. He said he had a bad dream about me. He didn't really want to talk about it but I prodded. He dreamed of trees and a car. He saw an ambulance and a stretcher. I haven't told anyone I'm dying so he surprised me. When he reads this, I want him to know that I love him very much and like I told him on the phone before we hung up, don't worry about me because God is going to take care of me.

Again, Solo, I love you. Say your prayers because God is very special.

If I tell people that God called me - that I wanted to go anyway, they wouldn't believe me, but I prayed for something and God blessed me. I'm happier than I've ever been, but don't feel I deserve it. But I want to do it myself. I'm going to be with the Lord because He is so sweet to me. This sucka talking about I'm too beautiful to die.

8:48 pm

On the freeway see money blowing around. Got out to catch a bunch of singles. Fun, fun.

I don't know what it is with this

sucka and doo-doo. I won't go into detail, but he smells butts. I'm trying to figure out why people would worship him. Like I'm thinking from past experience that he's some big bad only to find out that he's deeply entrenched in shit (pun intended) and not that bright.

But then God says he's a master of deception so he must be. In the past when dealing with him there was always a physical altercation. This particular situation is pretty shitty. Ha!

He's getting on my nerves. Jesus says his followers love him. What the? I think sometimes that I'm becoming vulgar. I remember God telling me weeks before this happened that I would be corrupted. I never expected this though. I don't want to be a sucka weirdo. I'm too stubborn for his crap.

He wants me to get mad and feel some stupid way about God. Nope. I see what he's doing. This is how he calls himself fighting with God. He can't beat HIM any other way but to try and destroy HIS plan. Just the way we expect God to be there for us, we have to try and do the same for HIM. This is my example - not allowing under rock dwellers to block my blessing.

He knew I didn't like him even back when I wasn't doing right. We bickered even then. I used to say "I did it"; the devil didn't make <u>me</u> do nothing. And it's true. If people did what they're supposed to do, he wouldn't be able to tempt us. He's not responsible for every bad thing we do, but there is stuff going on behind the scenes that we overlook. We can guess, speculate - whatever. But we don't know NOTHING, just like Job.

I won't act tough. Sometimes I'm talking to a friend and a wrong image or statement - or the voice will come and it throws me off or makes me nervous. I have no sense of privacy anymore. I just feel like everything I do is open.

Like basic things like going to the bathroom makes me feel bad - nervous. Last night, I thought the Lord called me again. I asked for more time. God told me to stick to what I am doing.

April 24th

So in trying to differentiate the voices, like God said, I have to wait and see what the voice is saying, which I have to remember to do because when they ask me something I just answer. God told me last night I don't realize how much I reveal when I talk to him.

Reminded me that I live in a world with people just like me who go through things too.

2:15 pm

I was sitting here thinking about the doo-doo. I was thinking about a story an ex-Satan worshipper posted online wherein he said that when Satan spoke of Heaven, he always referenced it as "that place". I was thinking of the way he's portrayed in pictures as an animal with a man's chest and a funky looking sheet wrapped around him. The statute is pretty close in resembling him only he's more bony in the chest. I was saying to myself people know too much about him. He says they don't see God and in so many words, he's there.

When you see a wicked man, know that at the moment he is performing his wickedness that God comes and strikes him. Just because you don't see the punishment doesn't mean that it doesn't occur.

"Master of Disguise. Could be sitting right next to you – a beautiful woman with long blonde hair, an old lady sitting on a train and trying to converse with you while you obviously read scripture."

Isa 64:7

And **THERE IS** none that calleth upon thy name, that stirreth up himself to take hold of thee: for thou hast hid thy face from us, and hast consumed us, because of our iniquities.

April 25th
9:18 am

Ok. He stung me this morning. Said something about them not caring about me if I have to go through this. I was just waking up - like had just opened my eyes about 5 minutes before. So I get up, get my coffee, and wake up. God reminded me of some things.

But as soon as I woke up this sucka was talking. Started off quiet. Then he's just prodding at me to try and get a reaction. He's trying too hard. Like can I be woke for twenty minutes? Damn.

God is so funny. HE's like, "I thought you said he wasn't going to dominate you." HE's like, "I can't believe you let this thing put you down."

I'm like, "You're looking at it. You can see what it is."

5 minutes later…

God said if HE was me, HE would punch that sucka right between the legs, kick him in the shin and when his head is bowed to the same height as mine, HE would grab him by the ear and tell him to get out. And he'd slam the door.

That just made me feel like something is in my room.
A voice says, "God put him out the door."

I'm thinking literally or figuratively? Because sometimes with God I have to wait and see what HE means. And the voice answered - literally. I don't know what to say. On one hand, I think I'm supposed to be scared but God is around and I wanna go back to sleep.

I don't react correctly in certain situations. Sometimes I think my reactions are inappropriate for the then current situation - whatever it may be.

So I was talking to him again though I'm not supposed to. I was saying that God isn't gonna let you do anything to me because fathers don't let things hurt their children.

Aye carumba.

So when you think about it, what does a father that loves his children do? Take care of them, protect them, love them. What is the relationship between fathers and their children when they love one another? Do we expect forgiveness, love, and understanding from our fathers? God has done all these things for me and I am NOT perfect.

But what are children supposed to do? Love their parent, respect them, take care of them, listen to them, and be obedient. But HE says if I want HIM to be God then HE'll just be God - if I'm good, HE'll reward me, if I'm bad HE'll punish me.

I wonder then what's the difference between a god and a father? They both punish and reward according to deeds. So HE makes reference to the gods of other religions that don't speak or hear their worshippers' prayers. But then I say they do speak. (I've always thought they were demons playing gods." HE says, no, they don't speak.

So what would God's children be like – would they be weak or strong? Not strong as in take on more than you can bear, but strong enough to bear what you can.

Our Father says good thing HE's not a cigarette or he would've got me by now.

Don't touch me.

12:02 pm

Got chased by a small dog while out jogging. I can hear the Lord calling me.

6:10 pm

I'm tired of him sitting over me and

talking like he's God over my head.

Back to sex stuff. I'm still very extremely happy. Don't want to rush.

8:38 pm

So acting like Jesus and in spirit trying to feed me or get me to drink stuff. That's never happened before today. First it was a white, bite-sized piece of something resembling bread. After I refused, he ate it as if to say there was nothing wrong with it. Couple hours later and it's a tall, dark cup of something. I don't trust it. I've never laid eyes on the Lord, but I know His spirit – or at least I used to before the "blindfold". I believe this may be Joshua though.

I remember the Lord sitting with me, being around while I go about, but I don't remember anything He told me. The effect of whatever He's said throughout the years remain, but specific memories are gone – what He's said dot for dot – gone. All I remember is Him being there.

HE says HE wants me to do this.

9:58 pm

Watching a video about a man that grew up in a devil worshipping household. He took the camera crew inside a witchcraft store and showed them statutes and prayer books with a book cover that showed Jesus being crucified. It was a prayer book, but this guy explained that there were no godly prayers inside. So all the time a body is not praying to God but thinks that they are. He said that inside the prayer book was nothing about the crucifixion or Jesus.

There's tons of these videos with people either going to hell, meeting the devil, Jesus, God – tons. These are the people we point at, shake our heads at or call crazy. There's even Muslims that have seen the Lord.

https://youtu.be/1KfgzDXe9ZY

To cause confusion, distract preachers, scare folks into believing God won't be there – all these things I never before thought about. I never thought of a devil worshipper in church or a demon purposefully wreaking havoc for distraction. We don't pay it any attention because we don't believe it can happen to us. Or we scoff and the first thing we say is, that's not real or this person is crazy. Now when you see it, wink.

This guy's testimony of the lake of fire is very vivid:

https://youtu.be/Fa5H1u5ow-U

So all in all, he has no repentance which is really sad. But I'm about to be done with this because it's really miserable when you think about it - not as miserable as people being misled into following a religion that's not about God.

Or being like me where you can't recall someone that you talk to daily. I can't remember the Lord and it drives me crazy because the devil plays like Him. There are moments - and I mean moments where I know it's Him, but I get paranoid. I know him especially when he won't pray and because he's so eager to 'lay hands on me'. I've been hearing about Joshua in physical form. In other news, the Lord and God are good.

April 26th
1:00 am

So the Lord says, "It all comes down to what you're thinking about."

I say, "Well, I'm thinking about shoes." (was on eBay)

God says, "He (devil) will take that shoe and turn it about and try to find a way to use it against you."

I can remember things about God, but it's like the majority of my Jesus memories - details - are missing. Was my memory wiped so that He couldn't be efficiently mimicked? Especially since He was the material factor in the trickery? The devil did ask me if He told me anything. Like what? Who the hell am I, Peter? Cause I mean for at least a decade I've talked to the Lord daily. I have events, memories, laughs that I can't recall.

10:53 am
    A few years ago, I dreamed that my spirit was with the stars. Above the stars is black. I remember seeing what I know were planets in the distance. I was spinning like head over feet. I didn't have control over my body but I wasn't scared. There was this beautiful music like angels singing. I knew exactly what it was. It was beautiful. I also remember feeling like I had gone as far as I could go because I had sin. I don't know that to be true, but that's how I've always felt. I am and was then ok with that. I was and am just grateful to hear that music.

An hour later…
He's complaining again. That ain't God.

    This whole situation I'm going through reminds me of the Story of the Cranes where Islam's prophet thought he had a message from the angel, Gabriel, but in reality the message was from Satan – trickery. I always admired how Muhammad confessed.

I don't know if I would've had the courage to do the same thing. I might have said something like, I made a mistake with the message, here's what it should say – not to save face, but credibility. Wouldn't want anyone to ask if I know who I'm talking to when I'm supposed to be leading a whole people toward God.

But he said it was the wrong message – came right out and admitted it. Just another prime example of devil trickery by acting like someone you trust.

Something about God and His 3 daughters

Surah 53:19-20

"Have ye thought upon Al-Lat and Al-'Uzzá and Manāt, the third, the other?"

Then, originally, the verses (known today as the satanic verses) were as follows;

"These are the exalted *gharāniq*, whose intercession is hoped for."

God told me to relate:

Now I heard a story once about jinn who I had always thought to be genies. Later in some odd reading, I found a tale which said that some jinn were passing by a reciting of the Holy Quran - heard it, liked it, and converted to Islam; that jinn who do not convert are in an army led by Satan.

So what I got from that was that jinn are virtually devils who if they did not become Muslim were essentially demons; that converted devils prayed with Muslims in fellowship, which was surprising again because I know how devout most Muslims seem to be.

So I went looking to see what MUSLIMS say…

Surah Al-Jinn 72:1-2

Say, [O Muhammad], "It has been revealed to me that a group of the jinn listened and said, 'Indeed, we have heard an amazing Qur'an.

IT GUIDES TO THE RIGHT COURSE, AND WE HAVE BELIEVED IN IT. AND WE WILL NEVER ASSOCIATE WITH OUR LORD ANYONE.

72:5

AND WE HAD THOUGHT THAT MANKIND AND THE JINN WOULD NEVER SPEAK ABOUT ALLAH A LIE.

Reader Reference:
http://www.islamreligion.com/articles/669/viewall/world-of-jinn/

Of course, one of the main discrepancies with Christianity and Islam is that Christ is the Son.

Surah 21:91

AND [MENTION] THE ONE WHO GUARDED HER CHASTITY, SO WE BLEW INTO HER [GARMENT] THROUGH OUR ANGEL [GABRIEL], AND WE MADE HER AND HER SON A SIGN FOR THE WORLDS.

And again at Surah 66:12:
AND [THE EXAMPLE OF] MARY, THE DAUGHTER OF 'IMRAN, WHO GUARDED HER CHASTITY, SO WE BLEW INTO [HER GARMENT] THROUGH OUR ANGEL, AND SHE BELIEVED IN THE WORDS OF HER LORD AND HIS SCRIPTURES AND WAS OF THE DEVOUTLY OBEDIENT.

Yet in Islam, the miraculous nature of His birth is down-sized and compared to the creation of Adam.

Let me make note of the fact that I am not Christian or Muslim. I believe in the One God, the Father, because He created us:

<u>Isa 64:8</u> But now, <u>O LORD, thou art our father</u>; we are the clay, and thou our potter; and we all are the work of thy hand.

<u>Mal 2:10</u> <u>Have we not all one father? hath not one God created us?</u>

I will say that "the Father" thing makes me feel a little sensitive. To think of God as a father, we would have to think that HE distributes love and forgiveness the same as a caring parent would do. Non-sensitive people (such as myself) see God as the balance - the judge of right and wrong. But when I'm frightened or I need something, I run straight for HIM with a sensitive heart. I guess it's up to the individual, but HE has been correcting me when I say "God".

I do believe that Jesus died for us. As a matter of fact, the Lord told me when He got stuck in the side that it "killed". I also believe in Him because God has never removed Him from me - ever. And God will wake me up out of my sleep at 3:26 in the morning to ask me why or what I'm doing. Meaning HE never said to me, don't talk to Isa or don't listen to Him. As a matter of fact, HE told me to "stay with Isa".

I questioned Isa once and God had fury with me - instantly.

Psalm 2:6-12

"Yet have I set my king upon my holy hill of Zion. I will declare the decree: the LORD hath said unto me, Thou art my Son; this day have I begotten thee. Ask of me, and I shall give thee the heathen *FOR* thine inheritance, and the uttermost parts of the earth *FOR* thy possession. Thou shalt break them with a rod of iron; thou shalt dash them in pieces like a potter's vessel. Be wise now therefore, O ye kings: be instructed, ye judges of the earth. Serve the LORD (GOD) with fear, and rejoice with trembling. Kiss the Son, lest he be angry, and ye perish *FROM* the way, when his wrath is kindled but a little. Blessed *ARE* all they that put their trust in him."

<u>The Lord would like to add that He loves us.</u>

5:23 pm

I couldn't go to the bathroom from him bothering me. God says that's how you know Lucifer because he thinks he can do and get away with anything

9:45 p.m.

Ok. I was doing something and the Lord instructed me. I remember HE used to do that. :-D

I confess that for a few weeks, He's been telling me to fast. I'll admit that I am not a faster. It's been at least four years since I've fasted. The experience helped. But it's something about fasting. I

don't know what it is. It's not that I don't care and food is not a big deal.
Angel, is it the smoking?

Whatever the case, He says that I will be fasting before I leave earth. It's wrong to say that too bad this isn't one of those times where I don't know who He is.

This sucka is glaring at the back of my head like I'm phony when I laugh. He's wearing my wig again.

So I just bought these shoes on Ebay. I go back to look at them and say, "Hmm, I don't know if I like the sparkles."

God says, "It's too late. You bought them."

I say, "Thank you, God."

It says, "Why do you thank God? You're the one who made the money."

11:20 pm

I would like to make note of the fact that when I laugh at something he says, it's mostly because (I'm stupid) or caught off guard at how much it speaks like human beings.

The Lord says to remember to walk in the light.

11:55 p.m.

God told me something then HE asked me if I remembered that about HIM. Yes, I do remember that HE tells me things before they happen to me or why someone is doing something or that they're about to do something.

April 27th
1:20 am

God says to me, "Don't ever trust him."

Like am I in danger of that?

"Ever," HE says.

10:00 am

Distractions, sure, but what's important to you?

I'm not supposed to talk to him but it's kinda hard when something is in your head. Like, Lord, excuse me for eavesdropping. I just happened to be walking past my brain and butted into the conversation.

As always, God always says the right thing. HE says my privacy has been invaded – and that calling HIM God seems pretty cold.

11:22 am

Out jogging - got chased by yet another

small dog. Lived in this area on and off for almost 15 years and never chased by a dog, never had encounters with a dog. Now after God told me about dogs, here we go. Now the big dogs are barking. The Lord told me to put the pistol on my belly. It's easier to reach. More comfortable to wear.

God cut my time from ten weeks to four.

7:45 pm

I'm overwhelmed. They take really good care of me.

11:24 pm

"Let's face it. You left me alone," it says.

I don't think I did. Whatever I did, I did on my own. But then the Lord came to help me repent.

I didn't actually get raped - not to me. Physically I mean, but sometimes my mental feels real effed up. Hurts a little. Embarrassed.

He's worse than a pest.

April 28th

He wants to weary God. He just told me this. Let's think about that. Can he weary HIM is not the question? It's the fact that he *wants* to. Think about it.

I wasn't there so I don't know what happened other than his responses in these verses which I had always before found to be a little…flippant…

Job 1:6-7

> **6**Now there was a day when the sons of God came to present themselves before the LORD, and Satan came also among them.
> **7**And the LORD said unto Satan, Whence comest thou? Then Satan answered the LORD, and said, From going to and fro in the earth, and from walking up and down in it.

By the way, what the heck:
Jude 1:9
"Yet Michael the archangel, when contending with the devil he disputed about the body of Moses, durst not bring against him a railing accusation, but said, The Lord rebuke thee."

So when Isa was tempted in the

wilderness I'll bet there were some conversations with the devil that were left out. The devil is lewd. I can just imagine what was said. God was with Him.

Psalm 1

1 Blessed *is* the man that walketh not in the counsel of the ungodly, nor standeth in the way of sinners, nor sitteth in the seat of the scornful.

2But his delight *is* in the law of the LORD; and in his law doth he meditate day and night.

3And he shall be like a tree planted by the rivers of water, that bringeth forth his fruit in his season; his leaf also shall not wither; and whatsoever he doeth shall prosper.

4The ungodly *are* not so: but *are* like the chaff which the wind driveth away.

5Therefore the ungodly shall not stand in the judgment, nor sinners in the congregation of the righteous.

6For the LORD knoweth the way of the righteous: but the way of the ungodly shall perish.

What makes him worse than the run of the mill serial killer/rapist?

- ✓ Murder
- ✓ Mayhem
- ✓ Grossly indecent
- ✓ Homicidal maniac
- ✓ Godless

"*Stalked everywhere...*"

He tried to whisper in my ear and I flipped out and hollered for God. I don't want him whispering in my ear.

Then I saw a girl lying down. She was glassy-eyed like she was in space. There was another woman sitting over her chanting and putting her in this trance-like state. I don't know where she was in her mind. Both of these women were young and looked like everyday people. I figured that the girl consented to being put in a trance, but I thought that maybe she didn't know what she was getting herself into.

I placed a cloth over her face and started to pray and the evil spirit drained out her ear like a gray liquid. She got up and started to curse at me. I told her that I thought she needed help, but still she was very upset at me. I thought about if it was myself and I was in the Spirit with the Lord and wickedness started to say some BS over me how mad I would be. She had my apology.

April 29th
11:30 am

I'm self-conscious now. My sense of privacy is gone. Now I have to remember if I feel a certain way did I feel like that way before this all happened.

But there are these very long stretches where there's nothing. Like after Joshua - the severe time - the trauma remained. But now it's not - heavy. So God allowed me to get my book. I didn't have to deal with more than I could handle, and again, I got my book.

I remember in the beginning God asking me something like did I want it to stop and me feeling guilty because I did, but I didn't, because I wanted my book. I was determined that my experience would not be nothing more than my own humiliation. I wanted him exposed. I felt guilty for wanting to deal with him to get my book. God helped me get my book.

Yes, I allowed myself to be further disrespected and God kept me from getting hurt. Because I wanted people to know what he did to me because it was WRONG! Just like with Job, he's always up to something dirty. But he wanted me to be mad at God and it *burns* him that I'm not cause all these weeks he's talking about God -

"If HE loved you HE wouldn't let this happen. They're lying to you. Why is HE letting me do this?"

"Ha! Sucka! Do you know how much God has done for me? I can take this hit, punk cause I love God!"

And he does this all the time! But that's okay. (wink) I'm gonna tell everybody what a pervectly, pervity, pervaceous weirdo he is. Absolutely pervtacular. Let me say for the record that he is a very nasty fellow. He's very old yet with the access that God has given him, one would expect a mix of things, but instead of using wisdom, he's 83% perv and 12% expose and 5% "what if this happened, what if Jesus tried to kill his Father" type fantasy BS. Which leaves me to the thought that where he cones from maybe that's normal.

Maybe God thinks we "normal" people are pervy with our dirty movies and...

1:42 pm

So at times after being asked a question or seeing something an involuntary thought will pop in your head. With me now when this happens I have to stop and think, do I feel like that? Keeping in mind that God knows what we think and do all the time yet I stand and wonder should I feel guilty about this odd thought or that odd feeling?

And this sucka stands by to try and make me feel guilt over a thought.

He says to God, "See that's why I said, let me talk to her."

I say, "You don't wanna *talk*. Pervoid!"

2:26 p.m.

I forgot it was the Sabbath. I can't remember nothing.

4:59 p.m.

I'm recalling a nightmare that I had over a year ago where I was sitting in my truck – at the time I had a small car, but in the dream I was sitting in an SUV, which I now have. I was in what looked like a state park because there were a lot of trees. I was in a deserted area for some reason and sitting in my vehicle when a man approached me. I knew instantly that he wanted to rape me, so I grabbed my pistol and he backed off. Now at the time I had the dream, I hadn't yet gotten my CCW.

I remember God telling me that he had raped an acquaintance, but he wouldn't get me. It was God that pushed me to get the gun. I won't reveal the acquaintance's name because she told this to me in confidence and also now because I realize that it's very embarrassing. Not only will people call you crazy but you feel touched. It's humiliating.

Some time later, she did in fact relate that the devil had tricked her. I thought it was just an unfortunate fact of god-fearedness that the devil will harass a believer. In fact, she told me about her experience some three months before I had my own experience – what I'm going through now. This dream never occurred to me because the man in the nightmare was an actual MAN.

7:02 p.m.

So I'm surfing the internet and come across some things about serial killers. There's a picture of a smiling victim.

I shake my head and I say, "How could somebody do that to another human being?"

The devil says, "When you have that body to yourself, you can do whatever you want with it."

So that, ladies and gentlemen, is what we're dealing with.

7:55 p.m.

So the Lord says to me, "That thing is going to play all kinds of games with you."

God says, "That's okay because he's going to be thinking all kinds of strange things. It has to remember that we're enemies. This is not one sided."

"Ha!" I say. Cause that's what he gets for messing with me! Then I say, "Lord, why is it going to play games with me?" Am I doing something?

He says, "Because you're not grabbing your collar." (something I do when I'm afraid or emotionally hurt)

April 30th
12:11 am

I can't even lay down without this weirdo circling. I won't say what's embarrassing to relay. I'm tired of his "make love" references.

9:39 pm

So HE's been telling me things before they happen and things I'll say before I say them. I think it's HIS way of reminding me that HE's ahead of me.

I flipped out in my car on the drive home from church. I felt very violated and violent. I mean flipped out to the point of spit and curses flying, punching the steering wheel – damn near doing a body flip. Pissed, okay, that this $#@%^ had the audacity to touch me.

But God has blessed me. He answered my prayer and that helps. He gave me the

WHALE!!

   I'm leaving for Florida in a few days.
Very happy about that.

May 1st

So I flipped out again this morning. It's been quiet all day.

Account #4
May 1st
Black female, 54 years

Q. Do you believe in God?

A. Oh, I love my Father.

Q. So will you tell me what happened?

A. It's been at least 30 years. One day I came down the stairs to find my sister just standing there. She was like, "there's something on my back. Get it off, get it off."
I'm like, there isn't anything on you.
But at that time, she was using drugs really heavy and I thought that she was just out of it. She kept saying, "There's something on my back. Get it off my back. Please pray for me."
Like I said, I didn't see anything but she was scared so I took her into her bedroom and prayed for her just so she would feel better. Now when I got to praying, she

started jerking on the bed. I went and got water to bless and came back to pray over her but found that she was asleep.

I started again to pray and read from the bible. I threw the holy water on her and she started to jerk again. Some time passed like that with me reading from the bible and then suddenly something jumped off of her. I don't know what it was. Maybe it was a demon. But the form was dark like a mist but it was formed. At that time instead of a bedroom door she had those beads, you know, the kind that hang in the doorway.

Well, it ran out the room through the beads and began to pace just outside the beads. It was staring at me but I couldn't make out a face just a black form. It was like "Bitch!"

Q. Were you afraid?

A. No. I never experienced anything like that in my life before or after then, but no.

Q. Then what happened?

A. I said, "Oh ok, so you think you're just gonna stand there?" I got up and walked through the beads while continuing to read from the bible and it ran to the front door and watched me. I knew the Lord was there to help. It was summertime and the front door was open. It ran through the screen door and out the house. My sister says that she doesn't remember, but I think she does. I know that is a time in her life that she wishes to keep in the past.

May 2nd
3:51 am

So I'm laying in bed and something is hovering over me and I see its shadow on the wall. The Lord said something to me about something wanting to do something, but I was pissed. I want to smack this dog and my nerves are kinda on edge. So I lay down on the couch and of course there's the shadow crouched below the fridge and I can see it from where I lay in the living room. Well, I think it again: "I wanna smack this —"

God says, "It wants in you."

So it wants to attack me. Now has claws.

It says it wants to crush my hip bones.

Me: "How?"

Instantly, I think something perverted. I heard some disgusting things I won't repeat.

It says it wants to hurt me. It wants to embarrass me.

I'll say it wants to get on my damn nerves. The claws surprised me. I'll say that

11:44 am

Isa said he (the devil) doesn't have anything - nothing. He has nowhere to go so he finds his comfort being with men.

12:33 pm

"You're not but one of the ones who cries out then tries to conjure another episode," the demon says.

Preachers message for the day: ***Conform - yield to the will of God.***

Why? Because man was not made to live independent of his Maker. To do so is Unnatural.

May 3rd
2:42 pm

So majorly there's been no sex stuff and when it is, it's in reference to Jesus. Why he would use Him? *shrug*

May 5th

"*My time is shorter than a midget on his knees.*" - Kahlif Berry

Feeling a little emotional right now. I don't think that God has done all HE's done for me just to leave me to a weirdo. I don't think so.

May 6th

On my way to Memphis and I hear him tell God that he needs more time - another 6 months. Really? I think God wanted me to hear that. As far as I'm concerned, he's had 60 days already. As old as he is, if he can't fail a 37 year old woman with the leeway that he's been given, is that my problem?

I'm extremely agitated as it is.

May 7th
1:47 pm

On my way driving to Daytona Beach, I flipped out again - weary, stressed. The devil is getting on my nerves. I haven't had sleep for 48 hours. I had doubts, wondered if God loved me. I was a little upset with HIM.

Isa reminded me that when I call for God, HE ALWAYS answers me.

I wondered if that meant that I should accept what was happening to me (emotional). He means that God is always there and sometimes we have to be there too.

I cussed it vulgarly and unladylike-ly for literally an hour - maybe more - then all was quiet. Made it to Daytona, but while on 95-S it just went at my left nipple. Felt very real, tongue and all. Freaked me out really bad. I had to clench both breasts in my hands to get him off. Got off at an exit for gas and it attached to my breast again. I was very, very upset – started to scream and cry and curse and almost went off the road. I'm pretty sure that was done purposefully – running me off the road attempt.

I felt very helpless and very upset to the point of shaking, near dizzy, light-headed. The morning before, God asked me to stop cursing which I didn't fret about. I curse like a sailor but so did the prophet Isaiah. About an hour before this particular molesting happened, God again asked me to stop cursing and I said I would work on it, but when it touched me I went off again. It was terrible.

Every day for nearly two months with him is taking its toll. I get reprieves –

let me say that - but he consistently asks me the same questions over and over. And he's very strangely curious about Isa. Isa says enemy. But the devil asks questions and is suggestive to the point of having an unclean interest in Him. Plus, he's disgusting.

He needs to be exposed. Isa has repeatedly told me not to talk to him. I guess I finally got it.

The pattern I've been noticing is if God or Isa says something to me, he comes right behind them and keeps talking like he's them and I respond, which is very annoying to me when I realize I'm talking to him. God told me long time ago to listen to what is being said before I speak. The problem is that he'll feed off a random thought. One minute I'm making a mental dollar store list then next thing I know I'm answering questions and talking or arguing at it.

And it will start off with "This is your father, God" or "Isa speaking". They never introduce themselves each time they speak to me but it still took me awhile to catch on.

2:30 pm

In my room taking a shower and God repeats to me what the hotel clerk said about not smoking in my non-smoking room and tells me that the man was serious about the $50 charge (HE knows that I would've lit a Newport on demand). About 15 minutes later, here comes the voice prompting me to smoke. Immediately, God reminds me to heed what HE told me. So here's it not only playing imposter - as God - but he will also come right behind God and try to take advantage. It wants to kill me. I want it away from me.

God took me from the gutter, closed my legs, gave me love, companionship, guidance. I am very hurt by this. It's been several days since I've been touched this boldly. When I complain it relents. But I don't like to complain to God because like I said before, I just can't see God being with me - helping me all that time, sending Isa to help me, keeping me fed, clothed, housed, money in my pocket, saying HE loves me - I hear HIM say this, I feel it in my heart - only to throw me away?

I don't see it. Then I think about Job and Jesus and Stephen who was stoned - I don't know. Of course God will help us but sometimes we have to trust HIM through craziness. I'm not frightened, but repulsed.

When this is read, I hope each individual takes some thing from this memoir that they can use. That's why it's here.

Yes, I love my Deity.

I sleep well.

May 10th
1:27 am

I don't know who I'm talking to most times. I mean, I'm worried about who's responding and because I know he's listening to what I say to God - prayers and everything. My cussing is still being worked on. The perviness has been all the way cut down - not to say he doesn't try. I've stopped talking to him like Isa told me to do A LONG TIME AGO.

7:11 p.m.

He tried his perv. I called God and he was instantly gone. I shouldn't have talked to him.

On top of that, my mouth…whew. It's okay when it's people - some odd Joe - but that one time with God and the baby broke my heart. I am so sorry. I was sorry then and the guilt ate me into a corner I think where

I took abuse from Joshua because of guilt. Once you hear God speak, you know you're not supposed to talk to HIM with a sharp tongue.

It's only been twice that I've heard it in two months, but I wish everyone could hear God's voice in their ear. It would stop a lot of nonsense.

Think about this. A man who's been in the penitentiary for decades comes out and is hard as nails. No one is phased. They say: So-and-so is hard.
And that's okay. We say, well, look what he's been through.

A police officer sees crime and murder everyday, deals with idiots. He's hard. People say, well, hey, look what he deals with everyday. And that's okay.

Earth is very old and God had been around for a long time. Look at what HE deals with on a daily basis. Who's hard now?

    Is that okay?

Think about it.

May 11th

"*Then Satan <u>entered</u> into Judas called Iscariot…*" – Luke 22:3

8:34 am

That's how I woke up this morning to a verse in one of my novels that I paid attention to but then I didn't really *consider*. He <u>entered</u> into Judas. We all know what that means.

He set Isa up.

On top of that, he's a RAPER! Rapist. But…my thoughts are sometimes inappropriate now. I won't be specific but I have to catch myself. Sometimes I'll be thinking one thing and end up somewhere weird or I'll say something to the Lord that I usually wouldn't.

The prowling is nearly gone. When I call God, HE comes straight away. This morning I imagined myself wearing concrete drawers.

It really upsets me that I have no power. Don't get me wrong, I enjoy calling on God to help me, but sometimes I wanna knock this sucka into next week all on my own. Especially when I was on the road on the way to Daytona and he did what he did with my breasts. That made me so mad that I was near foaming at the mouth. It's like someone hitting you and running before you can get your revenge.

> Moral of the story: I wanted to deal to get a story, but when I wanted the devil gone, I didn't know how to call for help. Don't talk to him.

Pray. Fight the devil when he attacks you. Job means that the wrong may not be yours.